CONTENTS

Chapters:

PREFACE

Except for a brief period under 'Alau'd-Din Khalji (1296 - 1316), the Sultanate of Delhi (1192 - 1526) was a militant state and warfare was the only justification of its existence. It had no roots in the soil. It had no polity commensurate to the country and its people, and virtually no administrative system. Religious fanaticism of which Barni's *Fatwā-i-Jahāndārī* is an eloquent testimony was the spirit of this government and loot and plunder its important source of revenue. There was no atmosphere for the growth of political institutions. The Delhi sultan ruled, as if, over an occupied territory without taking the masses with him in the matter of the governance of the country, and the people, therefore, viewed the sultan as an invader.

He had no cultural affinity with his subjects and ruled by sheer force. Whenever, therefore, the application or exhibition of this force was slack or weak, he was repudiated.

Chaos and confusion was already there and disintegration of this state had already set in during the reign of Muhammad bin Tughluq. The grand kingdoms of Vijayanagar and the Bahmanis had been founded and other distant provinces were also seething with unrest and preparing to alienate. Fīroz Shāh's policy to convert the Sultanate into a full-fledged Islamic state in the land of overwhelming infidels, who refused to betray their faith even in the face of harshest coercion, made confusion worse confounded. His death rang the last bell and the decade following his death was a period of complete anarchy. There remained virtually no central government worth the name and the forces of disorder and lawlessness were let loose.

The miserable state of affairs which prevailed at Delhi before the invasion of Timūr, in fact, needed a violent shock. Nothing except a shock could have restored order out of the chaos, and retrieved a state out of the anarchy. The invasion of Timūr completed the process of decentralisation of the unwieldy centralised despotism of the Delhi sultan who had been proved unworthy of the territories he possessed. Thus it was not a holocaust alone. In fact, it released the forces of reconstruction and reorganisation. It closed the period of chaos and confusion and ushered in an era of cultural renaissance in the country. It broke the flimsy and artificial Delhi Sultanate and established independent kingdoms in Gujarat, Malwa, Gwalior and Jaunpur which soon became veritable centres of great cultural activities, viz., literature, music, painting and architecture. It is a matter of singular importance that the greatest rulers of the pre-Mughal period in India came from these states which had sprung from the pieces of the Delhi Sultanate and had prospered on its ruin. The names of Aḥmad Shāh (1411-43) and Maḥmūd Begarhā (1458-1511) of Gujarat, Mahārāṇā Kumbhā (1433-68) of Mewar, Hoshang Shāh Ghorī (1405-35) and Ghiyāthu'd-Dīn Khaljī (1469-1500) of Malwa, Devarāya I (1406-22) and Kṛṣṇa Devarāya (1509-29) of Vijayanagar, Fīroz (1397-1422) and Maḥmūd (1482-1518) of the Bahmanī empire which also patronised such a great genius as Maḥmūd Gāwān (d. 1481), Ibrāhīm Shāh Sharqī (1402-40) and Husain Shāh Sharqī (1458-79) of Jaunpur and Raja Mansingh Tomar of Gwalior (1486-1516) may be mentioned by way of illustration. The period which followed the invasion of Timūr till the establishment of the Mughal empire by Bābur saw magnificent buildings (e.g., mosques, temples, tombs and palaces) rising from the ground at

Ahmedabad and Champaner; Chittorgarh, Kumbhalgarh and Ranakpur; Chanderi and Mandu; Vijayanagar; Gulbarga and Bidar; Jaunpur and Gwalior. They are rich in style as well as in number and some of them stand comparison with the splendid products of the Mughal age. Great schools of music and painting were established and great literary works were produced in these centres during this period. In fact, the Mughals built their cultural state upon the legacy which bequeathed upon them.

The masses sighed with relief; the fetters were removed and the freedom which now came within their grasp was utilised by them to review the situation and reorganise their house according to the changed conditions. With amazing dynamism, the Hinduism set to adapt to the change. The bhakti movement in medieval India was an outcome of this adjustment with the time. Such great savants of this movement as Kabīr (*c.* 1450-1518), Nānak (1469-1538), Vallabhāchārya (1478-1530), Chaitanya (1485-1533) and Mīrābāī (1498-1546) were, indeed, the products of the age to which they belonged. Fifteenth century, this way, marks the beginning of the cultural renaissance in medieval India, which not only completely changed the socio-religious pattern of the country and the people which proved to be most befitting in the changed environment, but also gave an altogether new complexion to indigenous arts. This great change paved the way for the Mughals; it gave them the basic material to shape their state and also to give form to their arts.

This work studies Raja Mansingh Tomar of Gwalior and the Tomar monuments (viz. palaces, gates, tanks etc) which have survived in the Gwalior Fort. Though it had a very short time span of 40 years (1486-1526), it was a potential precursor to the versatile and prolific architectural style of the Imperial Mughals of India.

Originally, published in 1982, it has now been thoroughly revised and updated with 14 text figures and 77 plates.

Professor (Dr) R Nath,
M.A., Ph.D., D.Litt
(Retired Professor & Head of the Deptt
of History & Indian Culture, University of Rajasthan JAIPUR)
Mob 08278687716
profnath@gmail.com
www.rnath.in

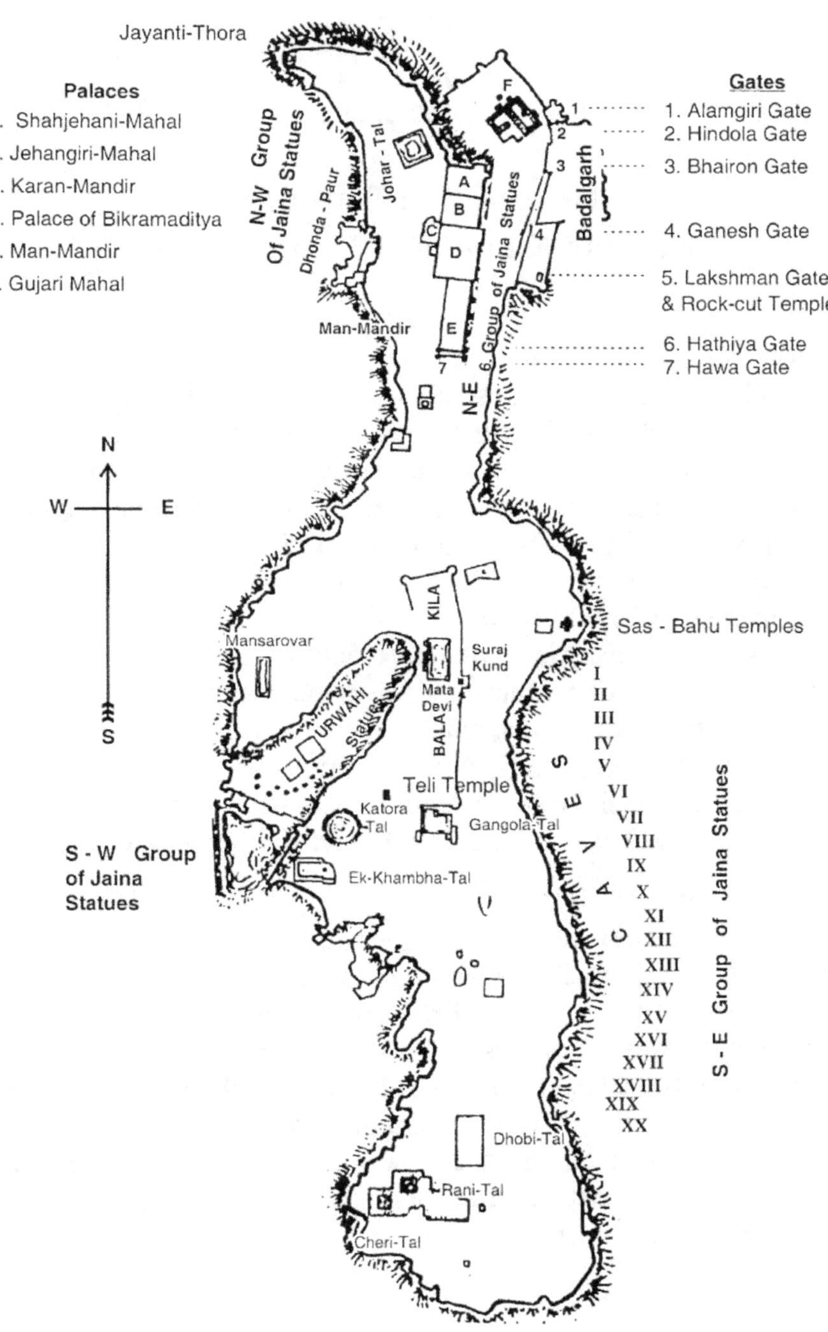

Plan of the Gwalior Fort and its Buildings (c.6th to 17th A.D.)

Historical Background:
Maharana Kumbha of Mewar (1433-68)

The first phase of art renaissance in medieval India set in with the accession of Kumbhā to the throne of Mewar in 1433. Not only was he a great patron of arts and literature, but he was also an excellent author, poet, musician and art-critic. He composed the *Saṅgīta-Rāja*, a grand treatise on fine arts which covered such subjects as saṅgīta (music), nṛtya (dance), nṛtta (acting with dance) and vādya (instruments of music) in nearly 16,000 ślokas and dealt with the theoretical aspects of fine arts (e.g., rasa) in exhaustive details. It draws largely on such basic, ancient treatises as Bharata's *Nāṭya-Śāstra* and has been made up-to-date with suitable additions, elaborations and illustrations. Kumbhā's epigraphs and contemporary works allude to his having composed, likewise, a treatise each on erotics and dramaturgy, viz., the *Kāma-Rāja-Rati-Sāra* and the *Nāṭakarāja* respectively; their manuscripts, however,

have not yet come to light. His four plays, a work on music entitled the *Saṅgīta-Mīmāṁsā* and a commentary on the *Saṅgīta-Ratnākara* entitled *Saṅgīta-Krama-Dīpikā* are also not available to us. He wrote an excellent commentary *Rasika-Priyā* on Jayadeva's *Gīta-Govinda*; his *Sūḍa-Prabandha* was an extension of this commentary. He also wrote a commentary on the *Chaṇḍī-Śataka* of Bāṇa, viz., the *Chaṇḍī-Śataka-Vṛtti*. He composed a work on the Kīrttistambhas which was engraved on stone tablets and fixed in the lower part of the Kīrttistambha of Chittorgarh; only a part of the first tablet has been found and is preserved in the Udaipur Museum.

He composed numerous poetic invocations to gods in various rāgas and tālas which are now contained in the *Ekliṅga-Mahātmya*. He was an accomplished musician and an unexcelled player on vīṇā and on account of his achievements in both the practical and theoretical sides of fine arts, he was known as 'Abhinava-Bharatāchārya' (New Bharata), which, in view of his masterly treatises on the subject, was not an exaggeration.

Kumbhā was also a great builder. He commissioned his able architect Maṇḍana to build the Fort of Kumbhalgarh and adorn it with palaces, tanks, temples and sculptures. The work began in 1443 and the edifices were finished in 1458. Kumbhā also built Achalgarh (Abu) and its various temples and tanks. He repaired and restored the Fort of Chittorgarh and built its seven poles (gateways). A large number of palaces, tanks and temples were also built in this fort. Like the Kumbhaswāmin temple of Kumbhalgarh (also called Māmādeva temple) and the Kumbhaswāmin temple of Achalgarh, a magnificent Kumbhaswāmin temple was built in the Chittor Fort. The most important of his relics, however, is the Kīrttistambha of Chittorgarh (which is erroneously known as the Jayastambha or the Victory Tower). It was built by his architect Jaita (Jaitra) with the assistance of his sons Nāpā and Panjā and was completed in v.s. 1505 (A.D. 1448). The tower which stands to the height of nine storeys and contains icons of gods and goddesses systematically arranged and indicated, so as to provide a veritable text of iconography personified in stone, is unique in the whole range of Indian art.

being similar! The style of its architecture is as magnificent as gigantic and vast is the project.

A large number of Vāstu-texts were also composed during his reign, mostly under his patronage. His architect Maṇḍana, elder son of Kṣetra (or Khaita), wrote as many as eight standard texts on Śilpa, viz.:

1. *Rāja-Vallabha*
2. *Prāsāda-Maṇḍana*
3. *Rūpa-Maṇḍana*
4. *Vāstu-Sāra*
5. *Devatā-Mūrti-Prakaraṇa*
6. *Vāstu-Maṇḍana*
7. *Rūpāvatāra*
8. *Vāstu-Śāstra*

Kṣetra's second son Nātha, younger brother of Maṇḍana, also wrote a treatise on the subject, viz., the *Vāstu-Mañjarī*. Maṇḍana's son Govinda wrote three standard works on different aspects of Śilpa, e.g.:

1. *Uddhāra-Dhoriṇī*
2. *Kalā-Nidhi*
3. *Dwāra-Dīpikā*

The creation of such a large number of texts during this period shows that there certainly was the need of a standard theory (śāstra) to strengthen and guide its practice (prayoga). Except for the Gupta age, no single epoch has such a large number of treatises to its credit.

Kumbhā revived the classical order of things, many of them in a way which would suit the changed conditions, i.e., by incorporation in the indigenous art of those elements which had been recently introduced into India, e.g., the arcuate modes of spanning the space in contradistinction to the horizontal system and the art of line and colour as distinguished from the art of mass and plane. Many lost texts were recovered and their standardised versions were produced. Scattered aphorisms were collected and compiled. New works were also written down and a vast literature on Śilpa was thus produced during his reign in Mewar by the family of architects whose ancestors had migrated from Gujarat; in fact, they are the product of the cultural milieu which can be conveniently termed as the Māru-Gurjara region (comprising the Southern Rajasthan and Northern Gujarat).

Kumbhā's efforts to revive and revitalise the ancient Indian arts, and to build the medieval arts upon the Śāstric dicta, mark the beginning of art renaissance in medieval India. It was he who laid the foundation, prepared the ground and paved the way for Raja Mansingh Tomar of Gwalior who derived wholesale inspiration, and also, as it seems certain, invited architects, from Mewar; the sources of the art of Gwalior lie deep in these attempts of Mahārāṇā Kumbhā to revive and reform the traditional arts of India. And ultimately it was on these secure foundations that the Great Mughals, Akbar and Shah Jehan, built their architectural style.

Raja Mansingh Tomar of Gwalior (1486-1516)

While the Delhi sultans remained busy with their own problems and embarrassments practically during the whole of the 15th century, the provincial kingdoms, now and then, enjoyed peace and prosperity which greatly promoted cultural activities. The first phase of art renaissance had its due impact upon the neighbouring states of Mewar and set things moving. The initiative was utilised in different ways in different regions, though the underlying trend to derive inspiration from the indigenous traditions of art remained the same.

The threads of the renaissance[1] were picked up, soon after the death of Kumbhā, by Raja Mansingh Tomar of Gwalior which had also become, at the expense and discomfiture of the Delhi sultan, a powerful Hindu state of northern India. He ascended the throne in 1486 and, during his reign of 30 years, he devoted himself wholeheartedly to the patronisation of fine arts: music, architecture, sculpture and painting. Undaunted by the repeated invasions of Sikandar Lodi, which would have easily drained his genius into military channels, he invited the greatest musicians, architects, sculptors and painters to his court and the Gwalior Fort hummed with great cultural activity during his reign which marks the second phase of this great movement. Almost the whole of India was then feeling the impact of this cultural revolution and the raja was beset in an ideal setting. Such bhakti saints as Kabīr, Nānak, Vallabha and Chaitanya were his great contemporaries on the one hand and rulers and empire-builders as Sikandar Lodi, Babur, Maharana Sanga, Mahmud Begarha and Krishna Devaraya on the other.[2] His own contribution to the most important aspect of this renaissance, viz., fine arts, is unique.

Like his august predecessor Kumbhā, Raja Mansingh was also an accomplished musician and equally well-versed in *Saṅgīta-Śāstra*. He revived the 'dhrupad' style (as distinguished from mārgī) and invented a few new rāgas and, this way, he initiated Indian music into the Deśī style. He held at Gwalior a conference of musicians in which almost all great artists of the age, viz., Baijū, Nāyak Bakhshū, Nāyak Pāṇḍavīya, Deva Āhaṅga, Nāyak Mahmūd Lohaṅga and Nāyak Karan participated. Various rāgas and rāginīs were examined in minutest details, their form and number were standardised and the conclusions of the scrutiny were compiled in classical order in the work *Man-Kutoohal*. This was, in fact, a more ambitious project than the *Saṅgīta-Rāja* of Kumbhā, as the latter was only a revised edition of the available texts on the subject mainly based on the *Nāṭya-Śāstra* of Bharata, while the former was a critical enumeration of the available data which was made up-to-date by incorporation of the style of music and the rāgas and rāginīs which had been introduced into India during the last two centuries and also of the innovations which had been made during this period. It had drawn from all great ancient works of Indian music, including the *Nāṭya-Śāstra* and the *Saṅgīta-Ratnākara*, as well as from the works of Amīr Khusrau, the *Saṅgīta-Śiromaṇi* which was compiled under Bahādur

Malin at Kara-Manikpur in 1428, the *Lahzat-i-Sikandarshāhī* of Umar Yāhiyā and all those changes which had been suggested at the courts of Bengal, Jaunpur and Kashmir. *Man-Kutoohal*, in fact, was the most representative and the most up-to-date treatise on Indian music. An additional merit of this work lay in the fact that though a classical production, it was written in Hindi, the language of the people at large, to be easily intelligible to them.[3]

This way, Raja Mansingh founded a great school of classical music at Gwalior which soon became the greatest centre of this art in North India. It was in this tradition that the greatest of musicians of the medieval period, including such a kalāvanta as Tansen of the Imperial Court of Akbar, were trained. In fact, most of the Great Mughal's first-rate musicians came from Gwalior.

The raja attached equal importance to architecture. He seems to have constructed extensively; it is a pity that only his buildings in the Gwalior Fort have survived and nothing outside it has come down to us. But there are enough of them to give an idea of the style which came into form under the raja, with distinctive characteristics.

Malin at Kara-Manikpur in 1428, the *Lahzat-i-Sikandarshāhī* of Umar Yāhiyā and all those changes which had been suggested at the courts of Bengal, Jaunpur and Kashmir. *Man-Kutoohal*, in fact, was the most representative and the most up-to-date treatise on Indian music. An additional merit of this work lay in the fact that though a classical production, it was written in Hindi, the language of the people at large, to be easily intelligible to them.[11]

This way, Raja Mansingh founded a great school of classical music at Gwalior which soon became the greatest centre of this art in North India. It was in this tradition that the greatest of musicians of the medieval period, including such a kalāvanta as Tansen of the Imperial Court of Akbar, were trained. In fact, most of the Great Mughal's first-rate musicians came from Gwalior.

The raja attached equal importance to architecture. He seems to have constructed extensively; it is a pity that only his buildings in the Gwalior Fort have survived and nothing outside it has come down to us. But there are enough of them to give an idea of the style which came into form under the raja, with distinctive characteristics.

'Paurs' (Gates) and Tanks of the Gwalior Fort

Gwalior's is one of the most ancient forts of India and, as the epigraphical evidence shows, it is the most ancient of them. The earliest inscription recovered from the fort belonged to the Sun temple which was constructed in the 15th year of Mihirakula's reign, *c.* 530 A.D. It seems that the temple stood on the east bank of the *Suraj-Kund* where a Devi temple was built over its ruins in 1882. The *Suraj-Kund* itself is an ancient tank which has been repaired and restored from time to time. Excavated in rock and with built-up masonry embankments, it measures 350 feet (106.68 metres) in length, 180 feet (54.86 metres) in breadth and 40 feet (12.19 metres) in depth. In the centre is a small island-platform with a miniature Śiva temple, which is connected to the eastern bank through a bridge supported on pillars (Plates I and II).

The famous *Teli* (Teliṅgānī) *temple* was built by the Rāṣṭrakūṭa Dhruva (*c.* 790). The *Gangola-Tal* tank seems to have been an excavation of this period. It is in two beds, the upper one is only 12 feet (3.66 metres) deep while the lower is nearly 50 feet (15.24 metres) deep. A large number of inscriptions were found engraved upon its bed when it was recently cleaned and desilted.[4] The *Dhobi-Tal* also seems to have been excavated during this period.

The Rāṣṭrakūṭas were ousted from the region by the Pratihāras, most illustrious of whom was Bhoja or Mihirabhoja (Amoghavarṣa) who assumed the biruda 'Ādivarāha'. The rock-cut *temple of Chaturbhuj* was built during his reign; it bears two inscriptions dated in v.s.

932/875 and 933/876 A.D. respectively. The *Laksamana Gate* and the rock-cut baoli near it seem to have been built contemporarily. The most important of the Pratihāra epigraphs, viz., the *Sagartal Praśasti* (*c.* 875) was also found at Gwalior on the Sagartal and is now preserved in the Gujari-Mahal Museum. Three other inscriptions of the Pratihāras were found at Gwalior. This shows that they reckoned Gwalior as one of the most strategic places of their empire. One of them alludes to a palace of Bhoja in the vicinity and it seems that it stood at the site where, later, Raja Mansingh Tomar built the *Man-Mandir*. The Sas-Bahu temples were built in the last decade of the 11th century; there is an inscription in the larger one dated in 1093. Another inscription which belonged to the extinct *temple of Mahadeva* is dated in 1104. In fact, the fort played an extremely important part in the history of northern India and was always garrisoned and defended as an outpost by the paramount power.

Iltutmish, the first sovereign sultan of the Delhi Sultanate, captured Gwalior in 1232. He took it from the Urwahi side where he had an inscription placed on the gateway. It was seen by Babur in 1527; he recorded: "Above the Gate leading from the valley to this walled-well the name of Sultan Shihābu'd-Dīn Ailtmish (Iltutmish) is inscribed, with the date A.H. 630/1232 A.D." [5] Ferishtah also mentioned it [6] and his translator John Briggs personally noticed it *in situ* around 1825: "The stone and the lines are still to be seen." [7] But this epigraph was lost thereafter and Alexander Cunningham, though he frantically searched, could not trace it between 1844 and 1865. [8]

The fort remained in possession of the Turks until the Tomars captured it from them around 1394. The early sultans kept it as an outpost. The Khaljis, however, used it as a state prison. Khiḍr Khān and other unfortunate sons of 'Alāu'd-Dīn Khaljī, viz., Shihābu'd-Dīn, Abu Bakr Khān and Shādhī Khān were imprisoned here in the dark underground cellars situated at the *Dhondha-Paur*. The dungeons are now called the *Nav-Chowki Jail* (correctly, Nava-Chakra or nine-circuited prison). It was here at this place that they all were ultimately killed in cold blood. [9]

'Ibn Baṭūṭah, the famous Moorish traveller, visited Gwalior on 25 September 1342 and noticed the stone statue of elephant with its rider, on the *Hathiya-Paur* (Elephant-Gate): "At the gate of the fortress is the figure of an elephant sculptured in stone and surmounted with the statue of a mahout." [10] He again alluded to this statue on his second journey to Gwalior. This shows that the famous statue was a pre-Tomar relic and stood near the series of Hindu buildings on the eastern facade of the fort.

The Tomars captured it from the later Tughluqs and, taking advantage of the invasion of Timūr, they became independent. They repaired the fort and strengthened its defences.[11] It was during Mansingh's reign, however, that the fortifications were completely renovated, an outwork of the fort, viz., the *Badalgarh*, was built at its foot and the beautiful gateway, the *Hindola-Paur*, added to it. At least two of his palaces, viz., the *Man-Mandir* complex and the *Gujari-Mahal* complex and one of his administrative buildings, viz., the *Chaurasi-Khambha* (Assembly Hall of 84 Pillars) have also come down to us with most of their original fabric intact.

There was already a watch-tower on the extreme north-western point of the fort adjoining the *Trikonia Tal* (Triangular Tank). Mansingh built two additional watch-towers on the north side, the direction of the possible attacks of the Delhi sultan. They were pillared pavilions with such features as projecting oriel-windows, bracket-forms, overhanging chhajjas and superimposing chhatris (Plate III). The existing palatial structures of this area, which were largely built by the Tomars, were renovated and rebuilt from time to time, under Humayun, Sher Shah, Jehangir and Shah Jehan, whose names still cling to these mansions. The Scindias and the Britishers converted them to suit their military requirements; they have almost entirely destroyed their original plan and fabric and, unmindful of their art and architecture, demolished parts of them. Some residential blocks have been converted even into horse-stables! Grotesque tin-sheds, pipes and wires have been fitted into their texture. Stone surfaces have been crudely white-washed and impression of a beautiful architectural style has been eyerywhere covered, eloquently, by the typical modern bad taste (Plate IV).

Raja Mansingh repaired and renovated the *Dhondha-Paur* complex[12] on the western side and provided it with additional defences. Following the Khaljī tradition, the Mughals also used this dreadful place, viz., the *Nav-Chowki Jail* as a royal prison; the underground cellars with the impregnable defences of the fort were the safest for this purpose and no prisoner ever came out of them alive. The jailor of this prison lived in the suite which was built at the head of this complex; the rooms still bear typically Mughal stucco and painting designs and a hammām. The Mughal jailor was independent of the governor of the fort and was directly responsible to the emperor.

The *Urwahi-Paur* was also renovated and enlarged by Raja Mansingh as the *Urwahi-Paur* inscription testifies.[13] This small gateway overlooking the Urwahi valley was accessible only through a broad stairway cut into living rock (Plate V). It was essentially meant for the inmates of the fort to fetch drinking water from the wells situated in the Urwahi valley. The wall over the stairway has a number of curious mason-marks which include pentagon, triśūla, aṅkuśa, svāstika and arrow, such words as नवपक्षी and गरुड़ and a few names probably of the artisans, e.g., सुदर्शन पौत्र पुत्र केशव (one who is grandson of Sudarśana and son of Keśava), रामदास and सन्जीवन.[14]

The raja excavated a tank, viz., the *Man-Sarovar*, near the *Urwahi-Paur*. He also built a mansion on its bank but, unfortunately, this has now been reduced to a mound and only parts of the plinth, a few lintels and brackets, and water-channels have remained. The *Man-Sarovar* is still intact though due to the crevices, which have developed into its bed, water does not stand in it and it has now been dried up. Its northern and western embankments (Plates VI and VII) with regularly disposed chhatris at the cresting still give an idea of the original charm of this vast reservoir. The *Urwahi-Paur* complex overlooking the western side of the fort with the outlying green country and the picturesque Urwahi valley below, and the *Man-Sarovar* in the vicinity was an ideal site for a residential palace and it is a pity that its structures have almost completely been destroyed.

The raja excavated and built other spacious tanks in the fort. The *Rani Tal* (Queen's Tank) and the *Cheri Tal* (Maid-Servant's Tank), situated together on the south-western side of the fort belong to his age. The former is a spacious square tank with double stairways leading to the water on its eastern side. The latter is rectangular and smaller. Overlooking it on the northern side is a double-storeyed pillared pavilion (Plate VIII). Massivity is its distinctive characteristic. This shows that these tanks were not only meant to store rain-water but also to provide pleasure-retreats and probably picnic-resorts to the people. The *Katora-Tal* (Plate IX) also owes its origin to Raja Mansingh. It is a circular tank, hence the nomenclature 'Katora' (= Bowl). It is 150 ft (45.72 metres) in diameter and 23 ft (7.01 metres) in depth. Like other tanks, this has also been excavated in living rock. Double stairways have been provided on the eastern side; below the set is a dalan. In the exact centre of the vast tank is a double-storeyed circular tower (Plate X) standing on the rock plinth. Each storey is composed of eight circular pillars. The upper one is protected on all sides by a circular chhajja which is similar to the one used on the chhatris of the *Man-Mandir*. The tower is crowned by an elongated dome which bears traces of glazed-tiling. All this belongs to the style of Raja Mansingh. Tomar. This is something novel in the otherwise simple water-tank; not only is it a beautiful feature in the body fabric of the tank, it also seems to symbolise the concept of art to stand over and above the deep waters of harsh realities. Though an integral part of it, it outshines and over-stays in full bloom like a lotus flower. Similar is the idea of the *Ek-Khambha Tal* (Tank of One Pillar) which also has a monolithic sand-stone pillar crowned by a square four-pillared miniature chhatri in its centre (Plate XI). It has a cupola and āmalaka finial (Plate XII). Here too its incarnation is guided exclusively by aesthetic consideration and it is not the least functional. This is also a spacious tank irregularly rectangular in plan measuring 200 ft (60.96 metres) on the longest side and 80 ft (24.38 metres) on the smallest. While the *Katora-Tal* is defunct, this tank retains water throughout the year.[15]

4

'Chaurasi Khambha' (the Hall of 84 Pillars), Gwalior Fort

Situated in the neighbourhood of the *Hathiya-Paur* (Elephant Gate), slightly to the south of the *Man-Mandir*, this complex is made up of a large pillared hall with an imposing portal (iwan) attached to it on the northern side (Plate XIII), a broad deep double-storeyed, circular baoli (step-well) just on its southern side (Plate XIV) and a small pillared pavilion to its west (Plate XV). Originally, the pillared hall was open on all sides with raised āsana-paṭṭikās on the north. In fact, it is a double-storeyed building, the basement having been completely closed down though its entrance below the eastern porch has survived intact. It is rectangular in plan with ten series of eight columns each, composing the hall and two additional columns each in the eastern and western central porch, there being 84 columns in all (see Plan, Fig. 1), hence the nomenclature: *Chaurasi-Khambha* or the Hall of 84 Pillars. Thus there are 63 square bays in the hall, each having a plain flat ceiling supported on interconnecting beams. The western porch has been entirely destroyed and its two external columns also are no longer extant.

All the columns are circular with massive bases and shafts and heavy capitals, all of grey sandstone; they are plain and unadorned. In fact, the whole interior is plain and simple. The Hall was used as arsenal by the British during their occupation of the Fort. The columns were plastered over and white-washed, and serially numbered. All external sides were walled up and the interior was enclosed with four doored-entrances in the middle of the four sides. Only the vitānas (ceilings) of the central bay (marked A in the Plan) having a lotus design carved in the stone slab, and the eastern porch (marked B) which is a typical Hindu corbelled ceiling of overlapping courses (Plate XVI), have remained unchanged; the eastern porch (Plate XVII)

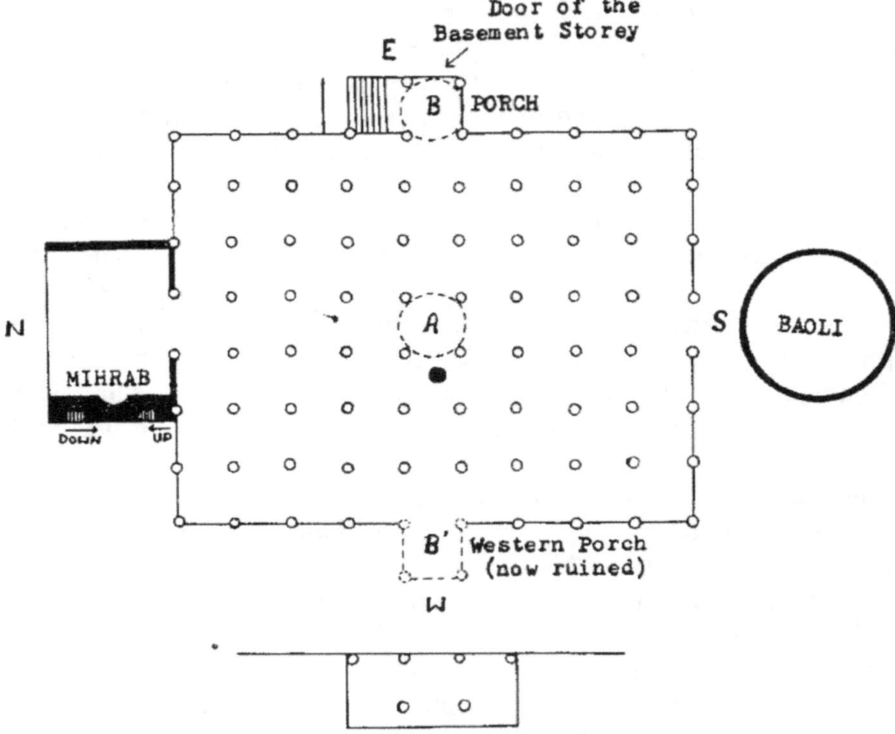

Fig. 1. Plan of the Chaurasi Khambha (*c.* 1500), Gwalior Fort.

and its stairs were also not disturbed. Later the building was used as a store-house and finally as a cattle-yard! Heaps of cow-dung still remain on the floor.

The eastern porch is roofed by a 'kamarakhī' dome (Plate XVIII) which rests on a square drum bearing merlons of stone. This dome is essentially ornamental as the ceiling of the porch is corbelled (see Plate XVI above) and it is only its filled-in exterior which bears the dome shape (Fig. 2). It could

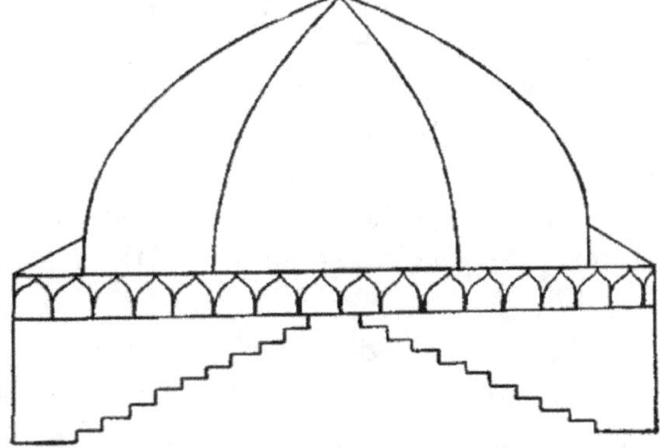

Fig. 2. Rough Section of the Dome over the Eastern Porch, Chaurasi Khambha.

have been plain and spherical instead of a six-sided 'kamarakhī' conformation and it is interesting to take note of the taste of the architect who chose this form to roof his corbelled 'vitāna'. It is slightly elongated while normally it could have been hemispherical resembling a cupola, or triangular, both such examples being available at the Qutub, Delhi, and the Ardhai-Din-ka-Jhompra, Ajmer, also over the corbelled vitānas. It has been plastered over; it seems that like the cupolas of the *Man-Mandir* chhatris, this too had been originally glazed-tiled in polychrome. This dome is a unique feature of this building.

No contemporary historical work of Raja Mansingh Tomar has come down to us, nor the buildings bear his epigraph. It is only their style which helps us to identify them. Its proximity to the *Man-Mandir*, the stone used in its construction which is similar in his other buildings, the design of the vitānas and form of the columns used in the hall, the adjoining baoli and the pavilion adequately show that the building owes its origin to him. It is quite likely, as may be surmised, that it was built to be used as Assembly Hall where, probably, the Great Conference of musicians was held and the *Man-Kutoohal* was compiled. In any case, an administrative building of the type of Diwan-i-am was the need of his regime and it is quite probable that while he built numerous other structures, an official building was also included in his architectural projects.

By far, the most important feature of the building is the stupendous portal which has obviously been added to its northern side at a later date (see Plate XIII above). In comparison to the yellow and white sandstone of the main building, the portal is made of red sandstone. It rises above the hall; in fact, it is a great iwan with a semi-vaulted soffit. It has a set of narrow stairways in the western wall accessible from outside. The upper one leads to the terrace, the lower which has now been closed, to the basement storey. There is a mihrab sunk in the western wall of the portal and, as it seems, this was used as a mosque. Near the mihrab is a Nāgarī inscription dated in v.s. 1586/A.D. 1529 which mentions Babur and Rahīmdād who held the Fort for him.[16]

Babur visited the Fort of Gwalior on 26 September 1528, about two decades after the construction of the palaces. He noted:

Riding on next day after the Mid-day Prayer, we visited the low hills to the north of Gwalior and the Praying-place, went into the Fort through the Gate called Hati-Pul [Hathi-Pole] which joins Mansingh's buildings and dismounted, close to the other Prayer, at those [buildings] of Raja Bikramajit in which Rahimdad had settled himself ... After visiting these buildings, we rode to a college

Rahimdad had made by the side of a large tank, there enjoyed a flower-garden he had laid out, and went late to where the camp was in the Charbagh.[17]

This college seems to have been built on the *Gangola-Tal* where at a later date Jehangir erected a building which also had an inscription. Subsequently, however, this was destroyed. Babur's description shows[18] that Rahīmdād's charbagh was laid somewhere near the *Hathiya-Paur*. This garden is not traceable at present. The appearance of Rahīmdād's inscription in the portal of the *Chaurasi-Khambha*, however, shows that this building was adopted by him and, most probably, it was he who added the portal to the existing structure. There could not have been any other occasion for the carving of the inscription on its wall. Had he built the whole *Chaurasi-Khambha* himself, the fabric of the hall would not have differed so substantially from that of the portal. The Hall is certainly a pre-Babur structure. Iltutmish's Jami' Masjid had disappeared during the interval and there was no other mosque in the Fort when Rahīmdād captured it from Tātār Khān Sārang-Khānī. It is quite natural that the Mughal garrison needed a mosque and this, with the portal containing the mihrab denoting the direction of Qibla, fulfilled the need adequately. Its correct orientation and the distinctly marked out mihrab confirm the contention.

Cunningham mentioned another inscription of Babur in the Fort dated in A.H. 935/A.D. 1528,[19] but this is not traceable. The *Chaurasi-Khambha* bears another Arabic-Persian inscription on the exterior side of the stairway of the eastern porch. It is covered in relief in beautiful nas-khi (Plate XIX). It begins with Bismillah-al-Rehman-al-Rahim which is followed by kalma. The date 25th of the Moharram of A.H. 938/A.D. 1531 is recorded in Arabic syllables which follow the kalma. The rest of the epigraph is in Persian recording the construction of this public building by one Yār Muḥammad, son of Maulānā Bahlol Nālbanda Kābulī. Finally it mentions that this place is useful alike to the friend and the foe, meaning thereby that this place had a sanctity and it was used for dispensation of justice. It seems that the structure which was originally built by Raja Mansingh as Assembly Hall was first adopted by Rahīmdād who added the portal to it and then it was used by Humayun during the period he resided in the Fort. It was used as House of Prayer and also as a Hall where he held his durbar, heard petitions and dispensed justice. Hence the reference in the inscription.[20]

The basement storey is entirely closed. The structure shows that this too would be a pillared hall, the lower columns supporting the upper ones respectively. The height of the lower columns would be half of the upper ones, as it may be surmised. The sides are closed. There may be a number of rooms around the hall. In its original form this storey might have accommodated the administrative offices of the raja and served allied purposes. The pavilion situated west of the *Chaurasi-Khambha* has been restored haphazardly and gives a crude impression. The baoli (see Plate XIV above) on its south side, on the other hand, was a magnificent structure and still retains much of its original charm. It is circular, entirely built of stone, the main storey having 32 circular columns making up a beautiful dalan which rotates around, and overlooks the shaft of the well. Its perennial source has been dried up and it is now defunct. However, the fact remains that though a water-structure, and hence strictly functional, the architect did not lose sight of the aesthetic aspect and he has organised his material in an extremely beautiful way. It is the most important baoli of Raja Mansingh as the *Man-Sarovar* is his most important tank. The close proximity of this huge baoli to the *Chaurasi-Khambha* as an integral part of its scheme shows that both were built contemporaneously. The Hall was used as the Diwan-i-am; the baoli supplied water and also the cool retreat in leisure time. Without doubt, it derived its inspiration from the traditional baolis of Gujarat.

The greatest importance of the *Chaurasi-Khambha* lies in the fact that it was a forerunner of the typical Mughal Diwan-i-am which was, as a rule, an open pillared hall built separately, yet in close neighbourhood of the residential palace, generally near the main gateway.

'*Vikram Mahal*' and '*Kirtti-Mandir*,' Gwalior Fort

The Vikram-Mahal which is ascribed to Raja Vikramaditya (Bikramajit) (1516-26), son of Raja Mansingh, is situated just north of the Man-Mandir, attached to it, overlooking the north-east cliff. It is a small building composed of an oblong hall in the centre with a square room on either side of it, each one having a single oblong doorway on the western side. There is a small square tank in front of the central doorway. Curiously, the eastern facade of the building is plain and crude and it is almost entirely closed. It is surprising that while ventilation should have been provided on the eastern side, this has only a small opening which too does not appear to be original. In fact, the building as a whole also is very poorly ventilated.

The western facade, on the other hand, is very interesting. The central entrance is protected above by a beautiful slanting chhajja supported on exquisitely carved brackets; the chhajja covers it like an umbrella. Above it is another smaller chhajja which is supported by bolder and less ornate brackets (Fig. 3). As a whole, these two chhajjas along with their brackets impart a graceful effect to the otherwise plain and dull facade.

On the terrace is a square room on the southern side. It has a single entrance and regularly disposed niches. However, the stone construction is crude and entirely without decoration. Roughly plastered surfaces are almost repulsive. The only interesting and happy feature of this room is the composition of its crowning which is made up of four square slender chhatris at the corners and a

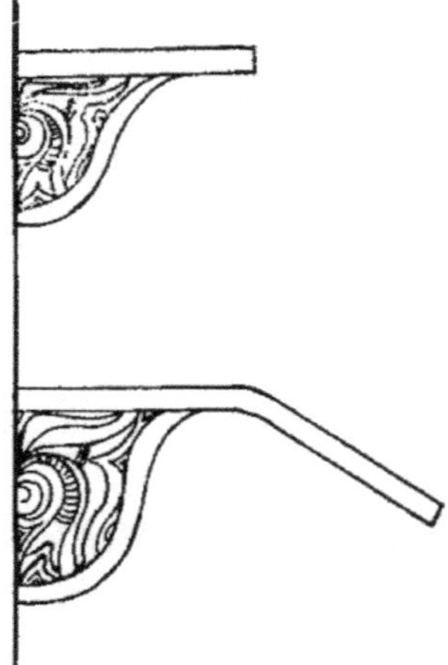

Fig. 3. Brackets of the Western Facade of the Vikram-Mahal (Section).

bigger chhatri in the centre, all of finely chiselled stone—marvellously set upon a pyramidal roof (Plate XX). They shine exuberantly over a frieze which bears carved stone merlons on all the four sides. Merlons are arch-shaped with ogee. This superstructure is an extremely tasteful feature of this building (Fig. 4).

Ceilings of all the four rooms are similar. Though they look to be wagon-vaulted, in fact, there is no arcuate system involved as the roofing has been done with the help of long beams of

Fig. 4. Figure of the Vikram-Mahal Superstructure.

stone. Each roof is slanting on the sides which appear to support the flat zone of the centre made up of stone beams which are visible. Two methods have been employed together to obtain this roof. Firstly, a large portion of the space which could not have been spanned by stone beams, has been covered above by corbelling reducing it to the central zone. Secondly, stone slabs have been placed over them on the interlocking system (Fig. 5). The sides have been plastered over to conceal

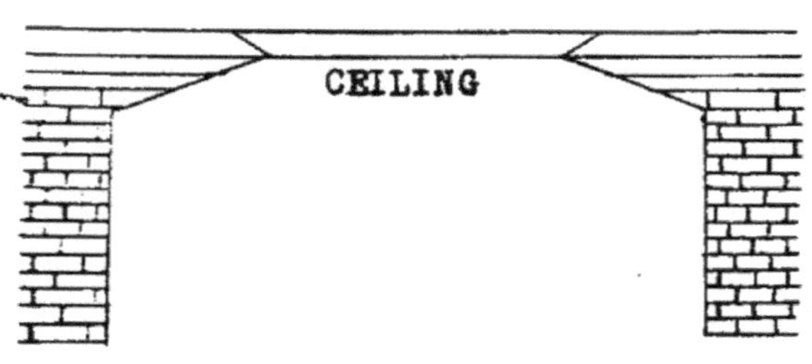

Fig. 5. System of the Ceiling, Vikram-Mahal.

the rough edges of the corbelled stones. Thus a strong and stable ceiling has been provided over a large hall which could not have been covered by stone slabs alone. This ceiling seems to have set the example for later constructions at Gwalior, Agra and Fatehpur Sikri. Like the organisation of the western facade and the superstructure, the manipulation of its ceilings constitutes a distinctive characteristic of this building.

The *Vikram-Mandir* (also called Vikram-Mahal) is popularly ascribed to Raja Vikramaditya (Bikramajit), son of Raja Mansingh. He ascended the throne after the death of his father in 1516. The Fort was besieged by Ibrahim Lodi soon thereafter. He is recorded to have captured the Badalgarh outwork. A bronze bull (Nandī) has been specifically mentioned as part of the booty. It is possible that it was taken from some Śiva temple which stood in the Gujari-Mahal complex at the foot of the Fort. Vikramaditya accepted the Lodi suzerainty and he died fighting for the Lodi sultan against Babur in the battle of Panipat in 1526.

There is no epigraph on the building. Any other Tomar record as to its history is also not available. The only reference of this palace appears in Babur's narrative. He visited the Fort in September 1528 and recorded:

> The buildings of Mansingh's son Bikramajit are in a central position on the north side of the Fort. The son's buildings do not match the father's. He has made a great dome, very dark but growing lighter if one stays awhile in it. Under it is a smaller building into which no light comes from any side. When Rahimdad settled down in Bikramajit's buildings, he made a rather small hall on the top of this dome. From Bikramajit's buildings a road (secret passage, precisely tunnel) has been made to his father's, a road such that nothing is seen of it from outside and nothing known of it inside, a quite enclosed road . . .[21]

Over and above the fact that Babur was a contemporary of Vikramaditya and he could not have erred in recognising and naming the building correctly, the secret passage from this block of structures going to the *Man-Mandir* still exists and confirms his description. It seems that tradition has preserved the name *Vikram-Mandir* correctly though the building has undergone overwhelming changes, beginning from Rahīmdād who had, according to Babur, settled down in this palace, to the British and the Scindias, and consequently there is very little original left in its fabric. As it stands today, it is more or less a patch-work.

The *Kirtti-Mandir* which is also called *Karan-Mandir* is a four-storeyed palace of much larger dimensions. It occupies the highest ground in the Fort, just west of the Vikram-Mahal. Tradition ascribes it to Raja Kirttisingh, grandfather of Raja Mansingh, who ruled from *c.* 1460 to 1480. Babur has not mentioned this palace specifically; probably he did not visit it. It is also likely, and possibly more likely, that on the eve of his visit, the palaces north of *Man-Mandir* were interconnected and enclosed within a single wall and the whole of it was then known as the *Vikram-Mahal*.[22] There is no other source available to us to examine the historicity of the nomenclature. The fact, however, stands out that the palace occupies the highest and, without doubt, the oldest of the palatial sites in the Fort and the name preserved by tradition may not be erroneous.

The two underground storeys are almost closed. They are dark and infested with bats. Curiously, the upper basement suites have a beautiful set of Mughal hammāms with furnaces, cascades and waterfalls, water-channels and lily-ponds and storage tanks. The arrangement of running water is so elaborate that there seems to be no doubt as to its being a cold-bath establishment. Walls have beautiful painting and stucco decoration in polychrome, in geometrical and arabesque designs in typical Mughal style exactly resembling the Fatehpur Sikri examples. These hammām-apartments show, beyond doubt, that the Mughal governor resided in this palace and it was he who had these suites constructed for his pleasure. The renovations in the basement area might have been done, thus, some time towards the end of the 16th or during the 17th century. Lower basement area is full of fearful dungeons.

The interior of the ground floor was completely renovated by the British who converted it into an office-cum-store. There is nothing original left inside it. The upper storey (this being the uppermost in the four-storeyed mansion) has, however, retained much of its original plan and disposal of rooms, verandahs, open courts and service quarters. The whole has been divided into several suites, each being self-contained with its own open court, rooms, stores, balconies and service quarters. Beautiful jharokhas for enjoying the distant vistas have been intermittently provided. There are raised platforms in open courts for open-air assemblies of the ladies. The construction is such that, if desired, strict seclusion could be enforced and purdah observed. As the palace stands independent of any other structure, it is open on all sides and perfect ventilation is facilitated. One is deeply impressed, in fact, by the ability of the architect who has successfully tackled the problems of sanitation, ventilation and useful distribution of space, and has skilfully provided all the living comforts along with pomp and show and other aristocratic requirements. There are no loose fittings at all, like a modern airconditioner, and it is altogether an architecture which has been adjusted, nay exploited, to bring out the maximum convenience of living. This way, it is an ideal residential building and demonstrates the way feudal lords lived in medieval India.

Its eastern facade (Plate XXI) has some original features. Though the ground floor openings have been converted into ugly modern grilled windows, the chhajjas over three of them have remained. There was a panel, showing a pair of elephants posed on the sides of a vegetational motif, below each of these three windows (Plate XXII). Two are still *in situ*, the third one is preserved in the Gujari-Mahal Museum. The figure of the animal in each case is lively and impressive. This is a popular motif of panel-decoration on friezes of palaces in Mughal architecture, e.g., in the Agra Fort and, as it appears certain, the inspiration was derived from these examples of the *Kirtti-Mandir* which almost served as prototype.

The three oriel-windows which project on the upper storey provide this facade a beautiful impression. The side ones are two-pillared jharokhas with mañchikās given at the base which add immensely to the graceful effect of this composition. The central one is a four-pillared pavilion supported on finely carved brackets. It has a pyramidal roof. Originally, it was half-closed by jalis, two of which have remained. There are no chhatris on the superstructure which is conceived in such a way as to lay maximum emphasis on the central pavilion.

The northern edge of the palace has a semi-octagonal plan, the northernmost side having a set of two oriel-windows one superimposing the other and a beautiful chhatri crowning them—thus forming a unitary composition almost resembling a tower (Plate XXIII). The lower oriel has a beautiful mañchikā at its base. This is the most beautiful feature of the palace. Over and above its great utilitarian merit that it provides sitting space to jharokhas in two storeys and a chhatri in the third, admitting tempered and subdued light and fresh and free air in the former case, the architect has also succeeded, through this composition, in giving this edge a substantial aesthetic impression. Almost a marvel, it is representative of the lucid skill of the medieval builder who would not behave merely professionally like his modern counterpart, but would have several ingenuities to introduce into his production chiefly for aesthetic effect.

Jharokhas and oriels, pillared pavilion and chhatris, jalis and mañchikā bases are the main characteristics of this palace. It would be interesting to investigate the source of their inspiration. There is no pre-Tomar palatial construction in the Fort or in the nearby region as far as Agra, which might have contained these pleasing features to provide guidelines for the builders of the *Kirtti-Mandir*. It is important to note that these elements have appeared in their perfectly evolved form without the slightest hesitation, and there is no doubt that the architect who employed them in his creation was fully conversant with their usage. In the absence of any local clue to the query, one is naturally led to surmise that Kirttisingh invited the builders from outside.

Kirttisingh of Gwalior was a contemporary of Maharana Kumbha of Chittor (1433-68) who was a great patron of architecture and who built a number of palaces at Chittor and Kumbhalgarh. Particularly, his palace at the former place has such features as jharokhas, oriels, pavilions, chhatris and jalis. They have been used there with emphasis and prominence as integral part of the architecture. As it appears, the builders of the Gwalior palaces, during the reign of Kirttisingh and, in a greater degree, in the reign of his grandson Raja Mansingh, came from Mewar. The point can be examined better, and in greater details, with reference to the *Man-Mandir*.

'MAN-MANDIR'
and the *'Hathya-Paur'* (the Elephant Gate), Gwalior Fort

The most important monument of Raja Mansingh Tomar is the *Man-Mandir* which is a vast complex of residential suites. Though the raja's epigraphs are largely available in the Fort, particularly wherever he did some construction or restoration work, e.g., at the *Urwahi-Paur*, the *Dhondha-Paur* and the *Gangola-Tal*, curiously the Man-Mandir does not bear any inscription. There is no court chronicle either.[23] But the account of these buildings in the Memoirs of Babur who visited the Fort just twelve years after the death of Mansingh Tomar, and an allegorical description of the palace preserved in the poetic work *Chhitai-Charit* of Narayandas who lived at the court of the raja, help us fairly authentically to identify the palace and supplement the data. Babur went into the Fort on 26 September 1528/935 "through the Gate called Hati-Pul [Hathi-Pole or Elephant-Gate] which joins Mansingh's buildings [imarat] and dismounted, close to the other Prayer [time], at those [buildings] of Raja Bikramajit in which Rahimdad had settled himself".[24] Babur thus confirms that the palace adjoining the Hathi-

Pole was built by Raja Mansingh and there is no ground to question the veracity of its legendary and popular nomenclature, viz., the 'Man-Mandir'.

Babur had a taste for architecture and his sense of observation was extraordinarily keen. He has left a graphic description of the palace:

I visited the buildings of Mansingh and Bikramajit thoroughly. They are wonderful buildings, entirely of hewn stone, in heavy and un-symmetrical blocks however. Of all the rajas buildings, Mansingh's is the best and loftiest. It is more elaborately worked on its eastern facade than on others.[25] This may be 40 to 50 qari (yards) high[26] and it is entirely of hewn stone whitened with plaster.[27] In parts it is four storeys high, the lower two are very dark; we went through them with candles. On one side of the building (i.e., on the eastern facade) are five cupolas having between each two of them a smaller one, square after the fashion of Hindustan (projecting square oriel-window with beautiful struts). On the larger ones are fastened sheets of gilded copper (upon the cupolas). On the outside of the walls is painted-tile work, the semblance of plantain-trees being shewn all round with green tiles. In a bastion of the eastern front is the Hati-Pul, hati [Hāthī] being what these people call an elephant, pul [pole] a gate [hence the Elephant-Gate]. A sculptured image of an elephant with two drivers [precisely riders, fīl-bān = mahouts][28] stands at the outgoing of this Gate; it is exactly like an elephant; from it the Gate is called Hati-Pul. A window in the lowest storey where the building has four, looks towards this elephant and gives a near view of it. The cupolas which have been mentioned above are themselves the topmost stage of the building; the sitting rooms are on the second storey in a hollow even; they are rather airless places although Hindustani pains have been taken with them ... Next day (i.e., on 28 September 1528) ... we saw the imarat called Badalgarh which is part of Mansingh's fort.[29]

Babur's narrative shows that during the four and a half centuries which have passed since he saw it, the palace has undergone tremendous changes. As for example, the main entrance of the palace which, in all probability, was also a ceremonial gateway, was given on the western side. It exists no longer. The through passage which connected the rooms on the eastern side with hanging balconies and jharokhas have been closed down. The broad corridor which maintained a liaison between the main court and southern apartments too has disappeared amidst crude additions and renovations which have been done in the area.

Equally useful in this connection is the contemporary account of the palace given by the poet Narayandas in his Braja-Bhāṣā (precisely, Gwāliarī Hindi) work of poetry (Prabandha-Kavya, प्रबन्ध-काव्य) entitled *Chhitai-Charit* (छिताई-चरित).[30] Ratanrang and Devchandra enlarged, and probably completed, this work with the consent of Narayandas, contemporarily. The poet lived at the court of Raja Mansingh Tomar and composed this work at Gwalior about 1500. After the disastrous battle of Panipat and capture of Gwalior by the Mughals, Narayandas migrated to Sarangpur where he has recorded to have recited the *CC* at the Viṣṇu Temple in v.s. 1583/A.D. 1526. The work is a prema-ākhyāna (प्रेमाख्यान) or a long continuous love-poem of 1030 chaupāīs (चौपाई). The story is related to Deogiri (modern Daulatabad) and the conflict of its ruler Raja Ramdev (Ramchandra) with Sultan 'Alāu'd-Dīn Khaljī of Delhi (1296-1316). Chhitai is former's beautiful daughter who is married to Samarsingh. The main theme of the poem is love and Śṛṅgāric play of Chhitai, in faithful adherence to the tradition of such compositions.

In this work Narayandas gave an account of the raja's cultural activities related to architecture, painting and music. Thus, he graphically described the construction of his palace. This is an allegorical description; in fact, the poet has given an account of the *Man-Mandir* palace which was built during his stay at Gwalior and to which event he was an eye-witness. It is the *Man-Mandir* palace which he has described in the *CC* and it is this palace which faithfully responds to his description.

Narayandas noted:[31]

The raja (allegorically Raja Mansingh Tomar of Gwalior) invited architects and expert artisans of stone-work and commissioned them to build a palace. Guilds of śilpīns were brought to Gwalior to work on the project and a large section of the treasury was set apart for this purpose. Such skilful and experienced śilpīns as Lanku, Gigo and Gunadas took over the work. Under advice of the astrologer, its foundation was laid in an auspicious hour. The Kṣetrapāla (precisely, Vāstu-Puruṣa) was worshipped and his benevolent powers were invoked for the strength and long-life of the palace. Deep and broad foundations were filled in with the assistance of seven high-born nobles. It was a four-storeyed square palace with rooms and halls (disposed all around) and ornamentation largely comprising of glazed-tile decoration, e.g., in the figures of peacock. Wood and stone were used in the structure and various entertainment halls (śālās) were tastefully adorned with paintings in which various bright colours including spots of gold were used.

The palace rose to a great height and almost went into the clouds. On the terrace several pleasing features as balconies, oriel-windows (jharokhas), ornamental pavilions (chhaparkhats) and chhatris were built to enable the raja to have a view of the country below. Golden kalaśas (finials) crowned these pavilions and chhatris. Many vegetational motifs, e.g., banana tree, were depicted in carved stone and mosaic of polychrome glazed-tiling. The beauty of this marvellous combination of stone relief and coloured glazed-tiling baffled the beholder. Fifty-two ingredients were used to prepare the lustrous glazed tiles[32] which shone like mirror and gave a unique impression.

A wonderful Chitraśālā (Hall of Painting) was built. The courtyards (i.e., their facades) were inlaid with precious stones. The system of interconnecting corridors and stairways almost made up a wonderful maze. Rooms and halls were also provided in the basement area where it was always dark like night. The columns were gilded (polished gold) and exquisitely ornamented like jewellery, and swings were given between them. A sphaṭika (emerald) throne was made in the Assembly Hall of the raja. Chakwa-Chakwi and other birds, aquatic animals, e.g., fish and tortoise, and the fabulous makara were tastefully carved on the walls. They looked lively and composed an extremely beautiful ornament.

The Sabhā-Maṇḍapa (Assembly Hall) had a pond which was similar to the one built by the Pāṇḍavas at Hastinapur (as we come across its account in the *Mahābhārata*). Those who came to see this building did not rest and went about the palace looking at these beautiful things. The maṇḍapa (pavilion probably built in the palace-garden) was made of sandalwood and was extremely cool in the summer season. On all sides of this pavilion, rooms were provided in order that the raja may rest there in the rainy season. The garden had fifty fountains of gold which sprayed water throughout and presented a rainy season the year round.

The chhatris on the superstructure had melon-shaped domes and wooden doors. Parrots and other birds had made their home in them and they generally sat on the projecting portions of the wall which bore glazed-tile ornamentation. They chirped and chattered and created an extremely pleasing atmosphere.

A suite had a concealed tank; apparently it looked to be a platform but when one tried to approach it, he fell into water. It was so skilfully made as to baffle comprehension. The kitchen had been entirely done with turquoise-blue glazed-tiles which looked like the blue waters of the sacred Yamuna. All the suites and apartments had been arranged symmetrically (in several storeys) in accordance with a regular plan and arrangement. [33]

These contemporary accounts help us to identify the palace and to partially reconstruct its architecture, the original fabric of which was much disturbed by subsequent changes, mostly under British occupation of the Fort. It must be recounted with regret that they treated the medieval heritage contemptuously and, with little or no appreciation or sympathy for the art of the natives, let loose the forces of destruction upon these beautiful structures. Thus, James Fergusson who made an on-the-spot study of these palaces about the middle of the 19th century, noted:

Of these buildings, which so excited the admiration of Emperor Babur, probably little now remains. The Moslems added to the palaces of the Hindus and spared the temples and the statues of the Jains, we have ruthlessly set to work to destroy whatever interferes with our convenience, and during the few years we occupied the fort, probably did more to disfigure its beauties, and obliterate its memories, than was caused by the Moslems during the centuries they possessed or occupied it. Better things were at times hoped for, but the fact seems to be that subordinates and contractors are allowed to do as they please, and if they can save themselves trouble, there is nothing in India that can escape the effect of their unsympathising ignorance. [34]

The *Man-Mandir* was most ruthlessly treated. Sir Lepel Griffin thus noted in connection with the two rooms situated on the eastern side of the inner court, which even Gen. Alexander Cunningham, during his long stay in the Fort, could not have seen: "The opposite or eastern face is not perhaps so rich in scrolls and borders as the western but it shelters two rooms, by far the most artistic in the palace. I scarcely think that General Cunningham has seen these rooms; or if he has, it was when they were coated over with accumulations of Muhammedan chuna and Anglo-Indian whitewash. It is only the other day that I recovered them from the commissariat department who used them as a godown."[35] Such references are abundant in the various accounts and reports of A. Cunningham, J.B. Keith and H.H. Cole. Whatever had remained was further altered by the Scindias in the pre-independence decades so much so that the plan of the Hindu palaces which was drawn up by Cunningham *c.* 1862[36] has now been completely disturbed and only its main apartments have survived.

As it stands today, the *Man-Mandir* has no unified or symmetrical plan and, presently, it is a haphazard combination of a few courts, scores of halls, rooms and verandahs, corridors, interconnecting passages and stairways, service quarters and open terraces – arranged in multiple storeys. The original ceremonial gateway which was given, as has been indicated above, on the western side is no longer extant. The high enclosing wall of the palace on this side has also dwindled, exposing the double-storeyed set of apartments to view (Plate XXIV). Instead, a broad stairway which was built, most probably, during the British rule, on the edge of this side, leads to the main plinth of the palace. This is, in fact, the first floor in relation to the ground level of the Fort. As shown in the plan (Fig. 6), 'T' is a simple entrance room.

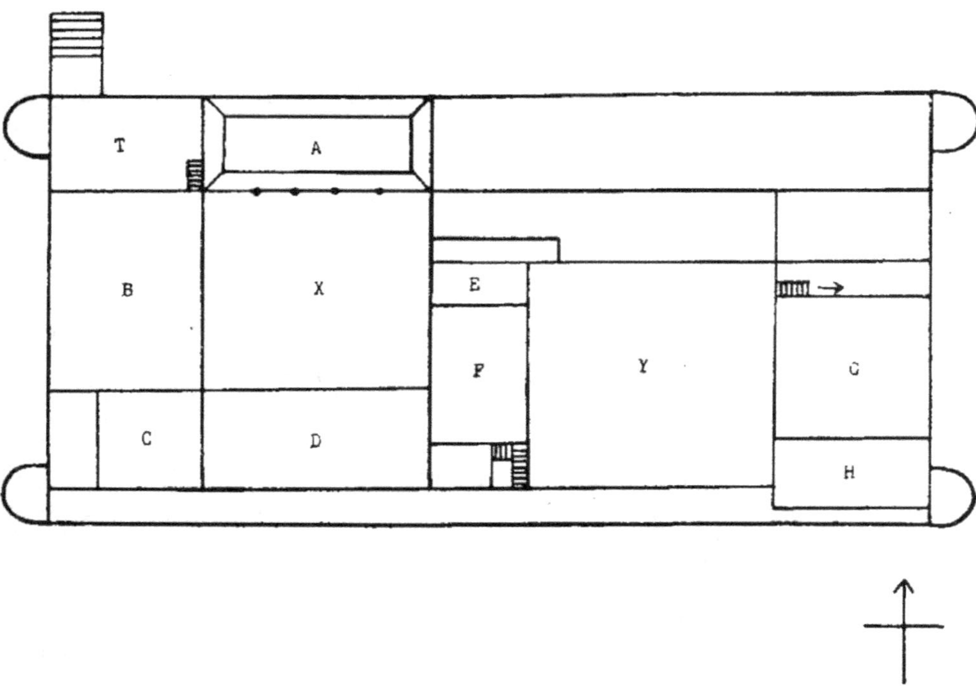

Fig. 6. Plan of the Man-Mandir (*c.* 1500), Gwalior Fort.

It leads into 'A' which is a beautiful oblong hall measuring 33'-11" × 14'-8" (10.34 × 4.47 metres). The pillars of this hall are in fact circular pilasters attached to curvilinear piers—all in richly chiselled yellow-and-white sandstone. Their bases and shafts are plain and simple but the massive overbearing capitals have been exquisitely moulded and carved. They corbel out as they rise like a 'chhatra' (छत्र), each zone bearing a beautiful design. These capitals are unique at Gwalior. Over and above their function—that they support a load—they bestow an extremely graceful effect upon this hall (Plate XXV). Its ceiling too is unique (Plate XXVI). Wagon-vaulted in appearance, it is a variation of the ribs-and-panels system. In fact, there is a rotating flat ceiling on all the four sides, in the nature of a rotating chhajja, supported on the capitals of pillars and pilasters, leaving an open space in the centre. Balustrades, filled in with jalis, then rise from the edge of this flat roof, each one resting on a pillar or pilaster. These balustrades supported the sloping ribs-and-panels ceiling of the hall (for plan and section, see Fig. 7). It

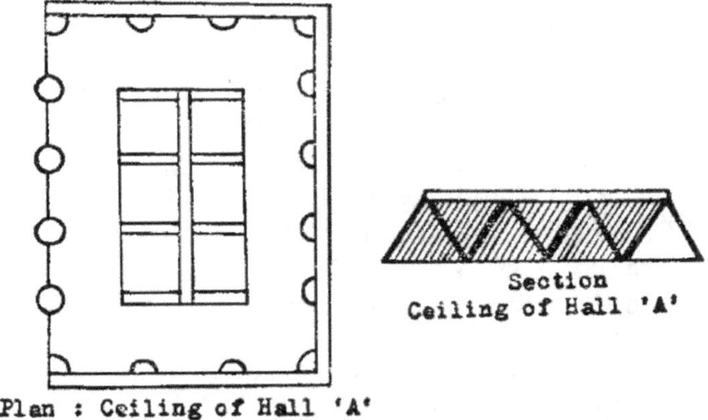

Fig. 7.   Plan and Section, Ceiling of the Hall 'A'.

has been very ingeniously conceived. Not only does it provide a ceiling to the hall, it also imparts an aesthetic impression to it. Curious is the fact that this roof is not on the terrace; as the hall is double-storeyed, it is inside the upper room the inmates of which could easily watch the proceedings or the performances going on in the hall below, through the jalis. This ribs-and-panels system, which is trabeated in essence, tries to adopt the typically Muslim wagon-vaulted ceiling in its own way, in stone. In c. 1500, it is structurally as unique, as it is ornamentally marvellous. Obviously, similar ribs-and-panels ceilings in the buildings of Fatehpur Sikri and Agra, built between 1565 and 1585 under Akbar, imitate the Man-Mandir examples. Of course, there is no upper room on the Akbari ceilings and they also lack the extremely graceful aesthetic impression of their Gwalior prototypes; there they are structural, pure and simple.

Hall 'A' opens in the court 'X' which measures 34'-9" (east-west) and 36'-6" (north-south) (10.59 × 11.13 metres).[37] Its facade (this being the northern facade of the court) has been gorgeously conceived (Plate XXVII). Three oblong openings of the hall 'A' have the same voluptuous pillar-capitals, being four in number, as are in the interior. These beautiful capitals (see Plate XXV above) overhang the openings as if they provide a shade (chhatra) to them. The 'śīrṣas' of these openings are filled in by exquisite jalis. The chhajja over them provides a rhythmic and harmonious horizontal line which pleasantly counteracts the vertical impression of the pillars. Over the chhajja on the second storey is a beautiful jalied balcony with an oblong opening. This too has been very impressively worked out. The jali-composition and, in fact, the composition of the hall as a whole is as chaste and exquisite as one may conceive it in ivory or wood; the whole of it and the graceful carvings are in stone and it seems incredible that the iron chisels and files could bring about such marvels in such a rigid material. This balcony is an architectural novelty, characteristic of the art of the Man-Mandir (Plate XXVIII).

On the western side of the court 'X' is situated the oblong hall 'B' which measures 33'-9" × 20'-6" (10.29 × 6.25 metres). It has a flat ceiling which is corbelled on all sides, reducing the span by about 4' (1.22 metres). Thus, by simple corbelling method (kaḍalikā-karaṇa), the breadth of the hall which measures 20'-6" on floor is reduced to about 16' over the corbels. It means that beams of 18' (5.49 metres) length have spanned the space. Each horizontal course of corbelling has a carved design, mostly composed of lotus-petals. This gives a pleasant effect to the otherwise plain interior (Plate XXIX). The traces on the main ceiling show that it had originally been painted.

This hall has a corridor (Plate XXX) measuring 2'-8" (81.28 cms) in breadth on its three sides; it is accessible through doorways on the smaller sides. The corridor also opens into the hall through square openings each measuring 10" × 10" (25.40 × 25.40 cms). They are three in one series, there being three series on smaller sides and five on the oblong side. This is an interesting feature. The openings certainly bring light and fresh air into the hall; over and above the provision of these ventilators, the corridor also has an interesting function. As an intermediary space between the hall and the exterior, it provides a sort of insulation to the hall, to protect it from the excessive heat and light of a tropical climate. It engulfs the hall on three sides and the latter consequently remains cool and comfortable. Exactly similar are the features of the southern hall of the Jehangiri-Mahal in the Agra Fort.

Obviously the Gwalior example has been imitated at Agra. The idea that this hall, as also the southern hall of the Jehangiri Mahal was used for puppet-shows and the ladies sat in the corridor in *purdah* looking through the square openings is far-fetched. There is nothing to sustain it and it is all hypothetical. It is necessary to keep in mind in such cases that whenever a residential palace was conceived, provision of maximum comforts of living was the basic concern of the architect and in such a hot climate as this, protection from the blazing heat and the dazzling light was his primary effort. Unfortunately, too much functional usage has been attached to this monument or that, almost entirely fancifully, to make the History romantic!

The facade of the hall 'B' (thus being the western facade overlooking the court 'X') has also been beautifully worked out. Unlike the southern facade which is in two storeys, this is only single-storeyed (Plate XXXI). The hall has three doorways which have, in fact, been made by horizontal beams resting on massive piers. But they are fitted in by semicircular jalis exteriorly, giving the impression of a semicircular arch, each (Plate XXXII). Interiorly, the stone slab over each opening has the shape of a seven-cusped engrailed arch. Both are ornamental features without any structural involvement. Jalis and carvings are again exquisitely worked out. Curiously, along with Hindu floral motifs, such typically Muslim designs as arabesques and stylised patterns have been used on a large scale. They combine perfectly harmoniously with the indigenous idioms. There are four circular discs in bold relief on the capitals of the four piers just below the chhajja (Plate XXXIII) which projects over the doorways; in these beautifully moulded and carved discs which bloom like full-grown lotus flowers culminates the beauty of the carved and jalied designs. At present, each disc has a vacant circular space in its middle indicating that something was originally there which, probably due to its extremely graceful sculpturesque impression, fell an easy prey to the vandals. The mural space above the chhajja up to the parapet has been divided into several horizontal zones which have been ornamentally treated with carving and glazed-tile decor. Series of blind ogee arches have been carved in stone and filled in, nay, applied upon by polychrome glazed-tiles, yellow, green and blue predominating. This typically Muslim glazed-tile work has most harmoniously combined with the indigenous stone-carving art and the facade as a whole presents a magnificent surface.

The eastern facade of the court 'X' is virtually closed, there is only an oblong opening, closed by jali, of the room 'E' which is set with the inner court 'Y'. There is, however, a chhajja on the first storey level supported by two beautiful peacock-brackets (Plate XXXIV). Over it is a balcony entirely closed by jalis which is also supported by moulded brackets. Here, too, the glazed-tiles have been inlaid tastefully with jalied and carved designs. The art of colour has gorgeously combined with the art of planes.

Hall 'D' is situated on the southern side of the court 'X'. It measures $35'-2'' \times 15'-5''$ (10.72 × 4.70 metres). It has three openings, the lintels of which are supported on massive, yet extremely graceful brackets. Over the openings is a wide projecting chhajja which is supported on six vyāla-brackets. Each vyāla (composite animal) is composed of lion's body and elephant's head[38] and obviously, it has drawn its inspiration from the indigenous art. It stands on its hind legs supporting a miniature elephant with its claws and also holding, simultaneously, a bud and garland motif (Plate XXXV). By far, this is the most artistic and beautiful bracket-form at the Man-Mandir. These brackets hardly take any load and are essentially ornamental. To impart a beautiful impression to the facade is the raison d'etre of this composition. Over the chhajja is a frieze of glazed-tiles. In the centre of the parapet is given a projecting rectangular mañchikā; this too adds tremendously to the aesthetic impression of the facade. As a matter of fact, this court has very pleasing glazed-tile ornamental scheme on all the four sides.

The ceiling of the hall 'D' is divided into five compartments with the help of cross-beams given in the breadth. Each compartment is supported on extremely luxurious bracket-forms which not only take the load but also provide the interior a gorgeous ornament (Plate XXXVI). Slabs have been used to span each compartment independently. This method has also been imitated though with a lesser effect at the Agra Fort, in a eastern hall of the Akbari-Mahal. A broad corridor on its south side connects it with other parts of the palace, as privately as the Lord of the House could have desired. It has four square openings for ventilation and a central opening for passage. There is a carved door-jamb and a semicircular architrave, both features being purely ornamental, each on the east and west walls of this hall. The carving work of the hall, as a whole, provides a pleasing ornament in the interior. All is stone work.

Room 'C' is situated to the west of the hall 'D'. It measures $16'-7'' \times 9'-9''$ (5.05 × 2.97 metres). The former is, in fact, a box-room of the latter. Such small rooms, locally called 'koṭhās' which were attached to large halls, were provided as a matter of residential necessity. The room is connected with the hall and also with the corridor. Particularly interesting is its arched ceiling. It is supported on two engrailed arches which have five cusps each (Plate XXXVII). These arches rise from two pilasters given in the middle of the oblong sides. In fact, the arches serve as ribs, intermediary space is filled in by circular slabs with key-system. This is also an ingenious way of spanning the space, in stone.

Court 'Y' is larger than 'X' and measures 41'-6" × 40'-6" (12.65 × 12.34 metres). Hall 'F' is situated on its western side. It is 17'-5" × 13'-9" (5.31 × 4.19 metres) in size. Another ingenious method of flat ceiling has been adopted here. In fact, as the extant examples adequately show, the architect of the palace was an extremely resourceful artist of his trade and he has taken recourse to a number of extraordinary methods of ceiling, both trabeate and arcuate. Thus, while he used simple cross-beams and corbelling in several halls, he also devised his own intricate methods of spanning the space. As shown in Fig. 8, two strong massive beams A and A' were inserted into the two opposite walls with their halves projecting

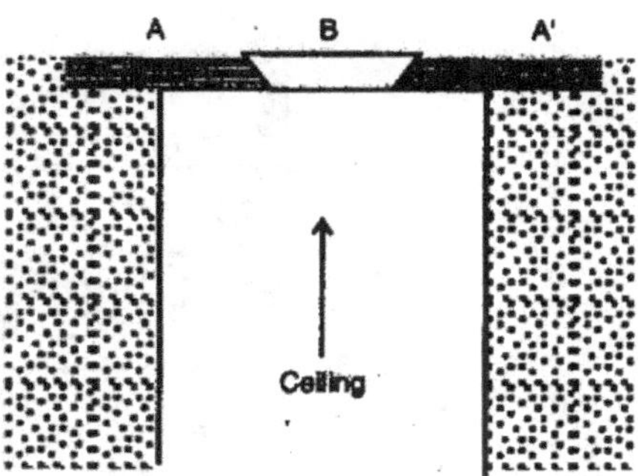

Fig. 8. Formation of the Flat Ceiling with Short Beams.

outside, their ends being chiselled slantingly. Another beam B, with its ends similarly chiselled on the reverse side, was placed upon the ends of A and A', where it was automatically supported without any cementing agent. Either the whole ceiling was spanned with the beams placed in this manner, or, as an economical measure, only a few beams were placed at regular intervals on this principle and the intermediary space was covered with slabs. This was crossed both ways skilfully to facilitate roofing by small slabs on either side. However, there remained a sad lacuna, viz., the cross-beams of the ceiling were visible from below and disturbed its harmony. The indigenous builder's inventiveness knew no bounds. He devised a solution. He prepared beams and slabs of triangular formation, e.g., slanting along their sides so that the latter will not only fit on the slanting sides of the former but will also join together below them to form an absolutely regular flat ceiling (Fig. 9, beams A, A, A and slabs B, B respectively).

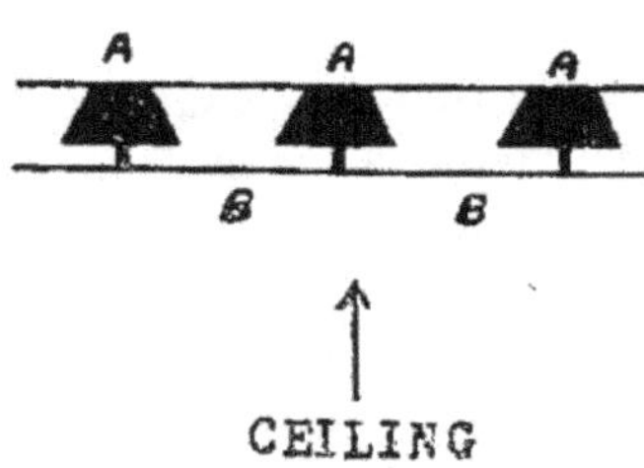

Fig. 9. Formation of the Flat Ceiling with Short Beams, Multiple System.

This system could be used in a number of variations without any

diminished effect or impression. The ceiling of the oblong hall 'F'
provides probably the best example in the Man-Mandir. Slightly projecting capitals, brought about by corbelling, support the main beams
on all sides on a svāstika-interlocking system as shown in the Plan
(Fig. 10 and Plates XXXVIII a and b). The larger beams a, b, c and

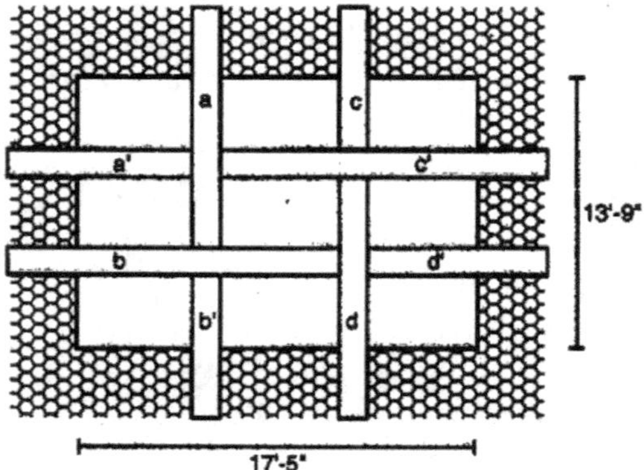

Fig. 10. Plan, Ceiling of the Hall 'F'.

d form an open svāstika and interlock the small beams a', b', c' and d'—
a with a', b and c; b with b', d and a; c with c', a and d; and d with d',
c and b—all the eight beams sunk adequately into the wall at one end.
Monolithic slabs have been placed over this framework, on all the nine
rectangles thus formed by the beam-work. The interlocking of beams
has made this ceiling extraordinarily strong and stable. This system
was later copied in the western hall of the Jehangiri Mahal in the Agra
Fort. Cornices bear beautiful carved designs composed mainly of series
of inverted lotus-petals. The central compartment of the ceiling has a
chakra and padma medallion.

This hall has three bracket-and-lintel entrances. Along with the
main brackets which support the lintel, beautiful ornamental struts,
forming a toraṇa, crown each entrance. This is an exceedingly pleasing
composition (Plate XXXIX). The chhajja is supported on six śārdūla
brackets which too have been as artistically carved as their vyāla
counterparts in the former court; the sculpture in each case is assertive
and effective (Plate XL). Inspiration in either case is indigenous. The
projecting stone chhajja is sloped and fluted exactly like 'khaprel'
(खपरैल) (Plate XLI), the baked clay pieces of which are used on the
huts in Indian villages since times immemorial, to throw off the rain-
water, and folk-art is obviously the source of its inspiration. Above it,
on the upper storey, is a beautiful four-pillared balcony (गोख) which

has three openings and a comfortable broad āsana for sitting—the whole supported on four brackets with a semicircular mañchikā in the centre and protected above by a chhajja. On the parapet is a slanting āsana-paṭṭikā crowning the balcony (Plate XLII) which is connected to the terrace. Carved designs in incised and low relief combine gorgeously with inlaid glazed-tile work as is the general scheme of mural ornamentation of the Man-Mandir. The western facade of the court 'Y' has been most magnificently composed with toraṇa doorways, khaprel-chhajja, mañchikā-based balcony and polychrome glazed-tiles set with carved designs; the effect of the composition as a whole imparts an extraordinarily graceful effect, which had been preconceived and anticipated. The raison d'etre of this great effort is architectural aestheticism.

The north facade of the court 'Y' (Plate XLIII) has no room or hall opening on it; they are no doubt there in a double-storeyed arrangement but they are closed by jalis. The lower set of jalis shows an underground passage, the upper set a hall. Jalis have geometrical designs which betray Muslim influence which is also discernible in various arabesque and stylised compositions used for mural decoration in carved designs. The 'khaprel'-chhajja which rotates on all the four sides of this court is supported on this side by a double set of simple vertical brackets; the lower set brackets have fine mouldings (Plate XLIV). Their sculpturesque parts which were loose fitted into them are no longer *in situ* and the hollow space leaves us conjecturing as to the real nature of these constituents. The mural space above the chhajja is horizontally divided into several zones; one bears kalaśa pattern, other a square cross pattern and so on, all carvings being gorgeously interspersed with mosaic of glazed-tiles mainly in yellow, green and blue colours. Yellow predominates in accordance with the climatic urge and consequential taste of the Indian people. The south facade is exactly similar except that instead of the double-storeyed arrangement of the north side, there is a running corridor 7′-11″ (2.41 metres) broad. This is only a part of the vast arrangement of corridors-and-staircases, the intricate network of which was originally spread in the whole palace like the blood-arteries in the human body.

Hall 'G' is situated on the eastern side of this court. It is square and measures 20′-6″ (6.25 metres) side. It has three brackets-and-lintel entrances towards the court and also three similar openings into its box-room 'H'. Hall 'G' is really the most beautifully designed in the whole Man-Mandir complex. It bears profuse carving work on all its mural surface which has been harmoniously and uninterruptedly facilitated by the design of the ceiling. This ceiling is also unique. In fact, there are two beautifully designed ribs at the groins, running across from one corner to the other, crossing each other at the apex of the ceiling where hangs a beautiful lotus-shaped pendant. There is a semicircular arch (with a semicircular ornamental extension), each on the four sides; these arches and the ribs constitute the framework upon which the ceiling rests, the intermediate space having been filled in by small slabs on simple vault-system (Plates XLV a, b and c). The whole load thus rests on the two ribs and the four arches which, together, make up the four vaults and, essentially, this is an arcuate method of roofing. In fact, this is a beautiful adoption of the typically Muslim 'Chahār-Tāq' method, in an extremely refined way in carved stone. The aesthetic consideration appears to have superseded the structural, but, in fact, the latter provides the basis for the former. Beautiful carved designs are not isolated motifs but belong to the scheme as a whole. Most important is the architect's conception to use a vault in stone in his own ingenious way. It is noteworthy that many types of flat ceiling of this palace have been copied at Fatehpur Sikri and Agra Fort during the early Mughal period but at least this was not followed anywhere else and it still stands unique. The four devāṅganā (heavenly damsel) sculptures which once adorned the central ribs on all the four sides exist no longer though their place is well marked out. The eastern side of this hall has niches and miniature openings; there is a jali in the central niche. It is surprising that no oriel ('jharokha' झरोखा) or balcony ('gaukh', गौख=गवाक्ष) has been provided on this side to give an open view of the countryside below the Fort and also for ventilation, and this side has been unusually and almost unwisely closed.

Room 'H' is attached to the hall 'G' like a box-room; it measures 18'-6″×10'-5″ (5.64×3.15 metres). The architect had a variety of ceilings in reserve and it seems that every time he would use a different type. The most noticeable feature of this room also is its ceiling. Square bracket-forms have been used at the corners which support diagonal pendentives over which the wagon-vaulted ceiling, with a flat-roof in the middle, rests. It has been so designed as to look like a great flower in bloom (Plate XLVI). Here too, it has been worked out entirely in stone which has been tastefully carved. One wonders at the novelty of his conception. It is noteworthy that the stone-carver has invariably accompanied the architect in the planning and treatment of every part of this palace; they go side by side together and share the work almost equally.

The eastern facade of the court 'Y' shows three graceful bracket-and-lintel entrances of the hall 'G'; the 'khaprel'-chhajja over them, curiously, does not have any bracket support on this side, i.e., on the east side (see Plate XLIV above). This shows that brackets on other sides were mainly ornamental; and horizontal courses over the chhajja made up of carved and glazed-tiled designs. On the parapet, in the centre, is a beautiful lotus-shaped semicircular mañchikā overlooking the court in an extremely noble and dignified manner (Plate XLIV above). It is only this way that architecture represents the manners and customs, and personality and character of its builder! The stairway on the N-E corner leads up on the terrace. Profusely carved and glazed-tiled, this court is, in fact, a rare example of the Hindu relief art beset most harmoniously and pleasingly with a typically Muslim colour scheme.

A set of beautiful apartments has been provided over the halls 'F', 'E' and 'A' which are at present accessible through the stairways given in the entrance room 'T' and in the S-W corner in the court 'Y'. These are private, almost entirely detached, rooms which overlook both the courts. Extremely airy and open, they seem to have been designed to suit residence in the rainy season. Such upper storey rooms are popularly called 'Chaubārā' (चौबारा) and, undoubtedly, it is with reference to such apartments that Narayandas noticed:

चंदन काठ कटाइल आना ।
ते ग्रीषम रितु हेम समाना ॥
चउबारे चउपखा सुदेसा ।
वरिखा बिरमइ तहां नरेसा ॥ १२६ ॥[39]

Openings of this suite whether 'gaukh' or 'jharokha' have beautiful jalis, almost invariably.

Service quarters of the palace are situated to the northern side of the court 'Y'. In fact, there is an intricate arrangement of open courts, verandahs, rooms, interconnecting corridors and covered, through passages on this side. Originally, the courts 'X' and 'Y' were connected with this set; now the whole system has been closed up and only a few openings remain here and there into which inquisitive visitors peep and wonder at the vast paraphernalia of the palace of a medieval lord!

A zigzag stairway, which takes its entrance on the S-W corner of the court 'Y', leads below to the basement. It is, at present, open only in two storeys. Most noticeable feature of this system of underground passages (Plate XLVII) and stairways is the wonderful provision of long overflying circular ventilators which carry light and air into the innermost parts very efficiently. This system too was copied at the Agra Fort where such ventilators have been most successfully used in the baoli situated in the Akbari-Mahal complex near the Bengali-Burj.

Much of the underground arrangement has now been closed up. There is a circular hall of 39′ (11.89 metres) diameter with eight massive round columns which are set 9′ (2.74 metres) from the wall and 9′ (2.74 metres) also from each other (see Plan of the Basement, Fig. 11); below it is a similar hall of the same size and conformation with a tank in the centre and other water-devices. Traditionally, it is known as Kaiser-Kund. No doubt, the water-devices, e.g.,

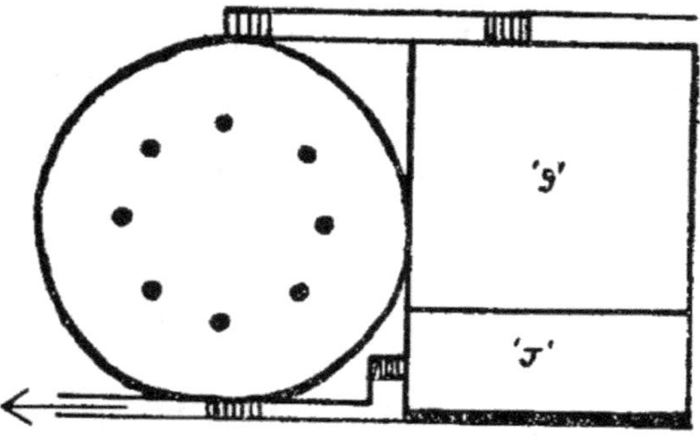

Fig. 11.   Plan of the Basement.

tanks, cascades, fountains and water-channels of the underground palace of the Jehangiri-Mahal at Agra Fort are far more refined and elaborate, and belong to a different order of things. The whole of it, as also the water-system on the terrace, have become defunct and it is not possible to reconstruct them for a stylistic study. The two halls 'I' and 'J' are situated adjacent to the circular halls; in fact 'I' overlooks the lower circular hall through jharokha-openings which also serve as excellent ventilators. It is square in plan and measures 21′ (6.40 metres) side. Here again, ceiling is its most important feature. It is composed of ribs-and-panels method on a simple plan (Fig. 12). The load is passed through the slanting ribs on the massive walls. This was probably the safest and the best translation of 'vaulting' in stone. The ribs are so set over the space on temporary centering as to interlock each other and the intermediary space is filled in by slanting slabs

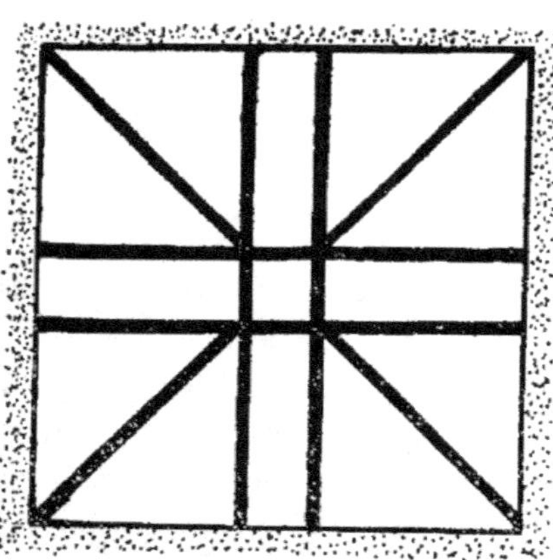

Fig. 12.   Plan, Ceiling of the Basement Hall 'I'.

placed over the ribs into their built-up edges (Plate XLVIII). Later, this system was followed on a very large scale at Fatehpur Sikri on account of its feasibility over large floor-areas, non-involvement of pillars, pilasters or brackets and greater stability and aesthetic impression. The hall is otherwise plain and, at present, crudely whitewashed. Long jharokhas given on the open side admit extremely tempered light and cool air. These basement halls were used, most probably, as summer retreat. It must be borne in mind that this part of the palace was never used as a state-prison, as fanciful guide-stories claim. As stated above, the prison was situated at the *Dhondha-Paur* Gate, viz., the fearful *Nauchowki Jail* and it was there that royal prisoners from the Khaljis to the later Mughals were kept and ultimately liquidated.

Hall 'J' is oblong and measures $17'$-$4'' \times 9'$-$9''$ (5.28×2.97 metres). Its ceiling is also very interesting. Pyramidal in form, it is made of central ribs and slanting slabs (Plate XLIX), on the same principle on which the ceiling of the hall 'I' was obtained. Camel's cart of Rajasthan had an exactly similar roof. It is essentially the village hut roof wherein the ends of two slanting bamboos are tied together, on either side, and support a horizontal bamboo across them; this is covered on either side by a roof of straw and leaves (called chhājana छाजन) (Fig. 13). The ceiling of the room 'J' has been obtained on an exactly similar system and, obviously, it has derived whole-sale inspiration from the folk-art. This ceiling has also been copied on a large scale at Fatehpur Sikri. The basement, as a whole, is devoid of that love of display of ornamentation

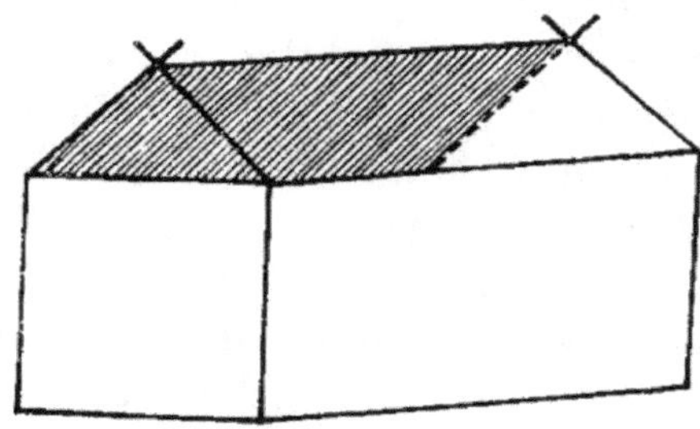

Fig. 13. "Chhappar" Roof of the Village Hut.

which runs riot in the main storey courts and apartments. In fact, the whole of it is mainly functional and provision of a little light, abundant coolness and a set of refreshing water-devices was the main concern of the architect.

The eastern facade of the Man-Mandir has six circular bastions, five chhatris of which are set at regular interval on the long terrace on this side. They have high, elongated cupolas which had been originally glazed-tiled in a colour which gave Babur impression of copper. Thus he noted: "On one side of the building are five cupolas having between each two of them a smaller one, square after the fashion of Hindustan. On the larger ones are fastened sheets of gilded copper."[40] Traces of glazed tiles have survived. These chhatris were crowned by āmalaka-and-kalaśa finials, only the āmalakas of which have survived. The two chhatris over the Hathiya-Paur gateway have a ribs-and-panels ceiling with a beautiful lotus pendant—all in stone art which is reminiscent of the chisels of the Khajuraho carvers (Plate L), though, technically, no devāṅganā sculptures are extant here. These chhatris are eight-pillared and circular in form; the upper chhajja and the slanting āsana-paṭṭikās which are interlocked one with the other, protecting the sides, are also circular and rotate all around uninterruptedly. Four square oriel-windows are set alternatively with the chhatris. They have cupolas, roofs and beautiful ornamental struts.

Unlike the plain screen of the terrace which crowns the parapet on the eastern side, the stone screen protecting the southern terrace has a beautiful cresting. It is broken at intervals by three chhatris (the one on the south-east corner, overhanging the Hathiya-Paur, being common to the set on the eastern side, and the chhatri of the bastion on the south-eastern corner not being extant) and three other wonderful structures. The central chhatri is closed by perforated stone slabs (Plate LI) in an extremely beautiful way. It is only in Rajasthan, where excessive heat, dust, winds and desert conditions much determine the way of life of the people, that such closed chhatris were used in the medieval period and this may point to the source of its inspiration. The other one is double-storeyed inside. Its soffit had been painted in simple green and white colours, much of which has survived (Plate LII). The beautiful stylised design is typically Muslim and it exactly resembles the one on the soffit of the Hathiya-Paur gateway. It seems that not only a Muslim glazed-tiler was employed by the raja, a Muslim painter was also patronised by him. Had this painting been done by a Hindu artist he would have also used his own motifs of indigenous flora and fauna and would have almost invariably depicted figural art composed of dancing dryads and nymphs.[41]

The other three structures are extremely interesting and important. Two with pyramidal roofs, having several tiers, each zone having a carved design, are 'chhaparkhat'-forms[42] in stone (Plate LIII) which overhang the southern facade of the palace gorgeously and impressively in the form of a closed oriel-window (jharokha) (Plate LIV and LI above). 'Chhaparkhat' is a folk word which combines 'chhappar' (छप्पर, thatched sloping roof) and 'khāṭ' (खाट cot—charpoy) or 'kāṭha' (wood); obviously, it has drawn its inspiration from the primitive village structure made of bamboo, wood and straw. It is a beautiful translation in stone of an essentially folk-element. This is confirmed by Narayandas who observed, contemporarily:

वादल घनह उठी घन घटा ।
रचे अनूप अटारी अटा ॥

छाजे   झरोखा रचे अनूपा ।
जिन्हहि उभकिते रहे जे भूपा ॥
कठछपर[43] सतखने अवासा ।
कंचन कलश मनहु कबिलासा ॥[44]

(The Man-Mandir palace, which was then under construction, rose high into the clouds and almost touched the sky. Several beautiful pavilions, viz., chhatris (अटारी), were built on its terrace where jharokhas (झरोखा) were also provided, through which the raja could enjoy the vistas. 'Chhaparkhats' (छपरखट) were built on the super-structure of this seven-storeyed palace and they were tastefully crowned by golden finials.)

These chhaparkhats have dual functions: to adorn gorgeously the superstructure of the southern facade of the palace, upon which they are set in the form of graceful oriels, as also to provide beautiful pavilions on the terrace on the internal side. In either case, however, the raison d'etre of their use is aesthetic impression rather than a usage.

Unlike these two chhaparkhat-forms which are square, the third structure has a circular conformation which is predominantly empha-sised by its round chhatra (छत्र, canopy) shaped superstructure supported on small graceful serpentine brackets (Plates LV and LVI). It has also derived its inspiration from primitive structures of India which had not only been used functionally in villages from the most ancient times but had also been depicted in the popular art. The best examples of the depiction of this form in stone come from the Lomas Rishi Cave (rock-cut) and the bas-reliefs of Sanchi and Mathura, dating from the 2nd

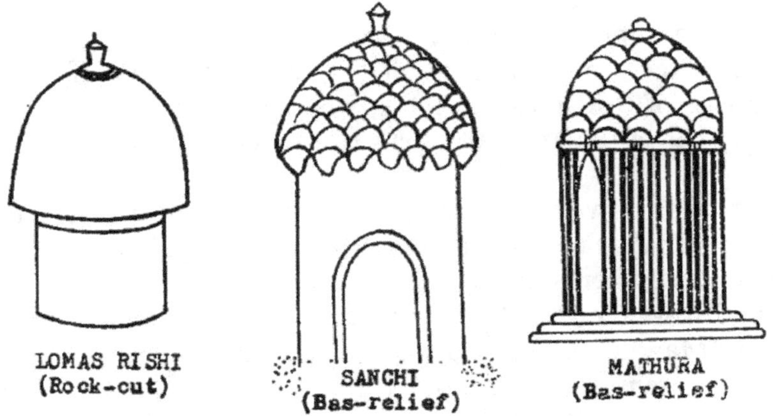

Fig. 14.   Primitive Structures (Folk-Art).

century B.C. to 1st century A.D. (Fig. 14). Its essential form is 'Bitaurā'

(बिटौरा) which is generally used in villages for storing cow-dung cakes (कण्डे). The round sloping 'chhappar' throws off the rain-water efficiently and adequately protects and preserves the contents. Built of wood, bamboo or reeds, straw, leaves and such easily available and equally conveniently manipulative material, it is a primitive structure that is in use in India since immemorial antiquity. The hermits also build a similar round hut with an opening and hollow space inside, as the bas-reliefs of Sanchi and Mathura depict. The form, in both cases, essentially remained the same. Narayandas had these structures in mind when he observed:

गोमट   खरबूजा   आकारा ।
तिन्हहि पवांरी जरे किवारा ॥१२७॥
चहुंघा खुटी कांच की भली ।
रहइ   परेवा   तहं   जंगली ॥
तिहं ठां सूवा सारो साखा ।
खुमरी बोलहि अन अन भाखा ॥१२८॥[45]

It seems, as the 'chhaparkhat' form also indicates, that the Tomar builder directly imitated the living primitive form, e.g., of 'Biṭaurā, rather than the art-motifs of Sanchi and Mathura. The folk-art of India was, until the beginning of the modern Nehru-period, a source of perennial inspiration to the artisans in all ages; while the Sanchi carver depicted it in bas-relief in two-dimension, the Gwalior builder reproduced the whole form in stone. Almost similarly thatched and supported, it is a unique structure in the whole range of medieval art. It is remarkable that kingship, nobility and aristocracy, in ancient and medieval times, did not hesitate to accept inspiration from the common ife of the people of India, in their pursuit of fine-arts. It is only recently that a trend to imitate exotic models in painting and architecture has taken ground, as a result of the adverse effect of one-and-a-half centuries of British rule in India, which has contributed to alienate a large number of Indian intellectuals from their own śāstric literature on the subject.

Traces of a few water-channels have remained on the terrace which show that originally there was an overhead arrangement of water-supply into various apartments of the palace. But these traces are too meagre, broken and scattered to help us to reconstruct the whole water-system of the Man-Mandir. Narayandas, in fact, recorded contemporarily that there was a system of intricate water-devices in the palace[46] but now this has all been destroyed. One simply wonders how the architect managed to raise water to such a great height in order to work these channels and tanks. Probably it was a system of relay-Rehanṭs in six or seven stages like the one which is still extant at the water-works of the Elephant-Gate at Fatehpur Sikri. The great baoli situated to the north-west of the Gujari-Mahal at the foot of the Fort might have adequately served as the source of this system. In fact, there are still some traces around the baoli which show that it was used to feed an elaborate water-system.

The southern facade of the palace (Plates LVII and LVIII) which roughly measures 160' (48.77 metres) in length and 60' (18.29 metres) in height has three semicircular bastions disposed at regular interval. The two are crowned by chhatris, the central one being closed, while the chhatri of the south-west bastion is no longer extant. The facade has been divided into several zones horizontally by cornices and string-courses, each zone having a series of its own design which is repeated, without the least monotony, along the whole length. Remarkable is the fact that the whole facade does not have a single plain surface which was the ideal setting for the Muslim ornamentalist; instead, there are several series of string-courses in stone relief, e.g., one is a corrugated (like the rings of āmalaka) cornice running across the whole span, the other is a miniature chhajja supported on miniature brackets etc.—which project forward and set harmoniously with sunk planes and zones. Manipulation of the play of light and shadow was the most popular device of the Hindu ornamentalist and the Man-Mandir provides one of the most successful examples.

The lowest design has a pair of makara-form (Plate LIX) in stone relief interspersed with glazed-tiles. Though stylised in an ornamental idiom, the makara is playful and lively. It is a wonderful phenomenon that this stone relief has set extremely beautifully with polychrome glazed-tile work and there is no conflict or confusion. Narayandas's description of these aquatic animals stands true to this depiction:

चकई चकवा कीए कडारी ।
जल कूकरी मटामरियारी ॥१२३॥
तिहठां श्रौर जिते जल जीवा ।
भरे भरति की साजति नींवा ॥
मच्छ कच्छ लघु दीरघ घने ।
ते सब चलहि द्रिष्ट कर बने ॥१२४॥[47]

Above it is a continuous series of blind toraṇas, each made up of a set of struts supported on a pillar-form which is, in fact, a pilaster. The whole of it is in high relief, the intermediary space is plain. A miniature chhajja protects this toraṇāvali (तोरणावलि) in a graceful way. A series of haṁsas, viz., haṁsāvali (हंसावलि) set in glazed-tiles, runs above it along the whole length. Then is a series of ornamental ogee arches which are also glazed-tiled. The broad frieze has several pleasing features such as elephants and lions, carved along with jalis; they too have been associated with glazed-tile art. Plantain (banana) trees have also been done in green and yellow tiles. The 'biṭaurā' structure overhangs this facade in the form of a semicircular oriel with a beautiful mañchikā-base, while the 'chhaparkhats' adorn it in the form of oblong oriels. They project forward gracefully and give an unprecedented effect to the superstructure. All the three are closed with jalis. It is surprising that the architect had such a wide variety of motifs and designs, and techniques and methods of ornamentation to employ on this facade. Its most remarkable feature is the total effect of glazed-tiling. The whole of it shines gorgeously and brilliantly without being dazzling; the stone relief work with which it is invariably associated tempers and subdues its glare and produces a pleasant and beautiful effect. Narayandas has made a mention of the use of glazed-tile work at Man-Mandir as follows:

बावन वस्तु मिलइ कइ वानी ।
अति अनूप आरसी समानी ॥[48]

But this is not a combination of 52 ingredients as he poetically conceived. In fact, this is 'Kāshīkārī' which was a complicated and elaborate system of fusing plaster tiles made of siliceous sand and lime overlaid with metallic oxides in specially built kilns.[49] It was most popularly used for architectural ornamentation in Iran in the Islamic period. The Muslim ornamentalist who was employed by the early sultans of Delhi took recourse to this art freely, in fact, as a typical Muslim form of mural decoration. Multan and Sindh were the earliest homes of this art in medieval India. By the middle of the 15th century, it was universally applied throughout northern India and also in the Deccan region. It is surprising that the builders of Raja Mansingh Tomar, the śilpīns Lanku, Gigo and Gundas as named by Narayandas, e.g.:

गुनी लंकु गीगौ गुन दासू ।
जानहि सिलप ते बहुत अभ्यासू ॥[50]

chose to take recourse to this form of decoration. It is a fact of singular importance. A great movement to accept, adopt and absorb various art inspirations which were introduced into India had already been set under Maharana Kumbha without taboos, inhibitions or even reservations so much so that even a śāstra for building mosque had been written down. Such typically Muslim features as arch, dome, vault, stalactite, squinch, geometrical and arabesque designs were being adopted in Hindu buildings—particularly non-sectarian—in Gujarat and Rajasthan. Dynamism of Indian art knows no bounds and no compulsion has ever restricted the scope of its inspiration or expression. It is at the Man-Mandir that all-absorbing liberal outlook of Indian art is writ large. Arch, vault, arabesques and geometricals have been used here without the least hesitation or reservation; it is, however, in the use of 'Kāshīkārī' on its facades and interior courts that this is most pronounced. It set the ideals of a national art for posterity and inspired such a great genius as Akbar, much of whose eclecticism may be ascribed to his worthy predecessor. This art has been very judiciously used with sculpturesque decor denoting a happy marriage of the 'plastic' and the 'coloured'. It is surprising that the art of line and colour has been set so marvellously harmoniously with the art of planes and zones; an art with a two-dimensional appeal has nowhere else been set in the third-dimension with such a superb and exquisite effect. This also shows the Indian builder's lucid capacity to adopt and assimilate foreign art inspirations into his own system almost indistinguishably.[51]

The arches used at the Man-Mandir complex are mostly ornamental; in a large number of cases it is either a single slab of stone shaped like an arch or two brackets or triangular slabs which together make up the arch-form. Mostly it is the ogee arch with a graceful curve at the apex. It is noteworthy that the ogee arch was used more popularly during the early Sultanate period than the typical three-centred oblong or four-centred broad arch; wherever the participation of the indigenous builder was decisive or even prominent, it is the ogee which has been preferred. Surprising, however, is the fact that not only the ogee, but several types of engrailing have also been experimented at the Man-Mandir. The most pronounced in this respect is the arch used in the southern annexe of the Man-Mandir. It is an ornamental ogee arch which has carved cusps along its intrados (Plate LX). Its appearance about 1500 at Gwalior is noteworthy. In a large measure, it anticipates the Mughal engrailed arch by more than a century.

A beautiful square chhatri (see Plate LX above) stands on the platform in front of the southern facade of the Man-Mandir. It has slender graceful elephant-brackets and a number of other carved designs and jalis. On its southern frieze is a Jaina Inscription in Nāgarī dated in v.s. 1661/A.D. 1604 during the reign of Akbar. It is doubtful that the 'karttā' of the epigraph also built this beautiful chhatri; it appears to be contemporary to the Man-Mandir.

The Hathiya-Paur (Elephant-Gate) is the main entrance of the Fort on the eastern side. It was so called popularly on account of a statue of elephant which adorned the gate for nearly four centuries. Ibn Baṭūṭah noticed this elephant when he passed by Gwalior on 25 September 1342: "At the Gate of the fortress is the figure of an Elephant sculptured in stone and surmounted with the statue of a mahout."[52] This shows that it was a pre-Mansingh and a pre-Tomar relic. Who installed it originally is not known. Surmises may ascribe its origin to the mighty Pratihāras who held the Fort for nearly a century, or to the Kachchhapaghāts. Babur, again, noticed it in 1527: "In a bastion of the eastern front is the Hati-Pul [Hathi-Pole], hati [hathi] being what these people call an elephant, pul [pole] a gate, [hence the Elephant-Gate]. A sculptured image of an elephant with two drivers (precisely riders, fīl-bān=mahouts) stands at the outgoing of this gate; it is exactly like an elephant; from it the Gate is called Hati-pul."[53] Ibn Baṭūṭah mentioned only one mahout. But his narrative generally lacks precision and is erroneous in details. Babur's account, in any case, is more reliable. It seems that the elephant had the image of a raja and the other of his mahout. Abul Faḍl also noticed this elephant: "Gwalior is a famous fortress and an elephant carved in stone at its gate fills the beholder with astonishment. It contains some stately edifices of its former rulers. Its climate is good. It has always been noted for its exquisite singers and lovely women; here is an iron mine."[54] William Finch was the last to see it in 1610. Probably it was appropriated and removed by the Mughal governor Muzaffar Khan (1628-47) who made large-scale alterations in the Fort.

The double-storeyed gateway has been most magnificently conceived (Plate LXI). Two bastions flank it on the sides. They are crowned by beautiful circular chhatris which are superior in composition to other four chhatris of this facade; they have finely designed pillars, bracket-forms and exquisite ribs-and-panels soffit (see Plate L above) in contrast to other chhatris which are plain and unadorned. The gateway has a lintel-and-brackets entrance. The exterior carvings which are exquisite and bold at the same time, however, give it the appearance of a semicircular arch. Two miniature ornamental oriel-windows crown this entrance on the sides. Upper storey openings are closed by beautiful jalis. The chhajjas in the respective storey impart the sheer verticality of the bastions a pleasing horizontal repose. The carving work has again been interspersed magnificently with 'kāshīkārī', mainly on the bastions. Massive stone pendentives have been used in the phase of transition of this gate to support a vaulted soffit which still bears traces of painting (Plate LXII) exactly similar to the one on the soffit of the central chhatri on the terrace. It may be reiterated that this is a typically stylised Muslim design. The glazed-tiler who did the facades and the courts and the painter who worked out such designs might have come from Sindh, Punjab, Delhi, Agra, Jaunpur or, most probably, from Mandu.

The Hathiya-Paur is an imposing ceremonial gateway which not only provides entrance but also gives a grand and magnificent impression. It is likely that Akbar learnt the principle to build stately gateways to cast impression of imperialistic grandeur and magnificence at Gwalior. It is remarkable that he had a pair of elephants carved in stone on the north-western gate of Fatehpur Sikri and also had their two statues installed at the Delhi-Gate of Agra Fort, both of which were, accordingly, called Hathiya-Paur. Thus noted the court historian Abul Faḍl with reference to the elephants of the Agra Fort: "At the eastern gate are two elephants of stone with their riders graven with exquisite skill";[55] and of the Fatehpur Sikri statues: "A masonry fort was erected and two elephants carved in stone at its gate inspire astonishment."[56] In fact, in his venture to rule India in an Indian way, he had much to learn from his predecessor native rulers; it is from them that he learnt 'jharokhā-darśana' and 'Tulā-dāna', for example. He was an ardent believer in the chakravartīn concept of the Hindu king and, accordingly, he followed all institutions associated with it. He even had a Sūrya-Puruṣa symbol personified in stone at Fatehpur Sikri in the so-called Diwan-i-Khas.[57] It is likely that when he sat to formulate fundamentals which later made up his architectural style, he derived large-scale inspiration from Gwalior which was situated in close neighbourhood of his capital and was a strong fortress which contained a royal treasury and an important town which had a royal mint.

The eastern facade of the palace (Plates LXIII and LXIV) which roughly measures 300′ (91.44 metres) in length and 100′ (30.48 metres) in height, has six bastions, in all, disposed with regular interval, two of which flank the Hathiya-Paur. The whole of it, like the southern facade, has been divided into several horizontal zones by cornices and string-courses (Plate LXV). The lower parts are generally plain—obviously to give emphasis to the superstructure, on the treatment of which the architect has given the greatest attention. Thus the makara series, though it is there on the gateway bastions, is not repeated on the main facade. The corrugated string-course has been used throughout its length. The series of blind toraṇas, viz., toraṇāvali (तोरणावलि) of this facade, unlike its counterpart on the southern side, bears beautiful glazed-tiled motifs in which plantain (banana) predominates. Some have the sun and chakra motifs. The colours used are green, yellow and blue. However, turquoise blue, the typical Muslim colour, is altogether absent. Series of blind ogee arches are also there though the haṁsāvali has not been used here. The whole of it is effectively designed, stone relief being magnificently combined with glazed-tile art. The ornamental treatment of this facade and its extremely beautiful effect has remained unexcelled even by the best examples of the Mughal art; the latter gradually tended to rely more on architectonic than on applied decoration as such, and it is only in the expression of this phenomenon that the Man-Mandir is left far behind the Mughal art.

In between the four northern bastions, the plain wall is relieved by three long, pillared projecting balconies, regularly disposed at the level of the lower storey of the bastion-chhatri, one in the middle of two bastions respectively. They rest on brackets with a sloping āsana-paṭṭikā in the centre and a chhajja over them. All these horizontal features set harmoniously with the vertical pillars and the bastions, providing a rare example of beautiful interplay of horizontal and vertical lines in the third dimension. These and the rotating balconies of the chhatris are accessible by a long through corridor (Plate LXVI) given in the thickness of the wall. It is also connected to the various suites of the palace.

The four bastions north of the gateway are crowned by double-storeyed circular chhatris which have plain pillars. It is noteworthy that the load, in fact, rests on massive piers which are concealed inside the structure of the chhatris and the pillars are only ornamental. The lower storey has been conceived in the form of a rotating balcony. The elongated cupolas were originally glazed-tiled traces of which have remained. Four oriel-windows with graceful ornamental struts have been used alternatively with the chhatris, one in the centre of two bastions respectively, crowning the parapet impressively. They are integral to the composition of the superstructure. They relieve the monotony of the plain wall and also the monotony which would have been there by repetition of the chhatris; their slender graceful forms in fact, set among the overprotruding massive bastions, on the cresting of the parapet extremely beautifully. The parapet is made up of large thin sheets of stone. Some are blind, while others have small jalied designs. The whole of it has been most beautifully designed. It is surprising that the Tomar architect could handle the skyline (Plates LXVII and LXVIII) in such a wonderful way in *c.* 1500, much before the Shahjehanian architect learnt to manipulate it at Agra and Delhi about the middle of the 17th century.

'Hindola-Paur' and 'Gujari-Mahal' Complex, Gwalior Fort

The *Dhondha-Paur* and the *Urwahi-Paur* are situated on the western side of the Fort. The former is built on a high rock which is accessible only by a footpath. It has a single gateway flanked by typical Tomar chhatris. There are sharp and crooked curves, steep rises and several trap-points to put the besiegers in a dangerously disadvantageous position. A continuous series of broad, long stairs further renders assault by elephant, horse and wheeled conveyance impossible. The *Urwahi-Paur* has a broad road, which leads up to the Fort, and it has comparatively larger space. Consequently it is more vulnerable to attack than other gateways. It was from this side that Iltutmish succeeded in storming the Fort in 1231. On the south-west is the inaccessible *GarGarj-Paur*. The eastern side has several gates on the winding steep road which rises from the level of the town to the level of the rock on which the Fort is built. Next to the *Hathiya-Paur*, when one descends, is the *Laksmana-Paur* (Pole). The rock-cut temple of Chaturbhuja built during the reign of the Pratihāra King Bhoja Ādivarāha is situated near it. It has two inscriptions dated in v.s. 932/A.D. 875 and 933/876. Then is the *Ganesh-Paur* (Pole) which was a great centre of Mughal activity during the 17th century, as the Laksmana-Gate was in the 9th. Motamid Khān, 'Ālamgīr's governor, built Nūr-Sāgar and a few palatial apartments near it in 1078/1667. The legendary shrine of Gwālipā situated in close vicinity of this gate under the overhanging cliffs, though ravaged over and over again, had survived and was finally converted into masjid by him in 1075/1664, as the inscription on the mihrab testifies. This is the only documentary evidence of the existence of the Gwālipā Temple. The *Bhairon-Paur* (Pole) comes next downwards. At the foot of the Fort is the magnificent Badalgarh-Gate which is also called the *Hindola-Paur* (Pole) (Swinging-Gate). The 'Ālamgīr-Gate was added to it as the exteriormost entrance by Motamid Khān in 1660. The Gūjarī-Mahal is situated in close neighbourhood of the Hindola-Paur and the whole complex was built by Raja Mansingh.

Khwājah Nizāmu'd-Dīn Aḥmed who compiled his *Tabaqāt-i-Akbarī* in 1593-94 recounts that shortly after accession to the throne, in 924/1518, Ibrahim Lodi decided to take Gwalior and sent a large force under Āzam Humāyun Sarwānī to besiege its fort;[58] he noted further:

It so happened that at this time Raja Man, the ruler of Gwalior, who had been distinguished above all his peers and neighbours for bravery and liberality, and had contended for years with the sultans of Delhi, had died and his son Ray Bikramajit [Vikramaditya] having succeeded him, had made great exertions in strengthening the fortress. The amirs of Sultan Ibrahim in accordance with his orders had erected a palace and every day assembled there, and attended to all matters of importance and made all efforts and endeavours to carry on the siege. It so happened, however, that *Raja Man had erected a lofty building below the Fort which surrounded the latter and was very strong and was called Badalgarh.* After a considerable time, the sultan's soldiers excavated mines and filled them with gunpowder and set fire to it, and the walls of the Fort having been blown down, they entered it, and that place was conquered. At that place they found a brazen bull which the Hindus had for years worshipped. In accordance with the orders of the sultan that brazen bull was taken to Delhi and placed at the Baghdad-Gate. Up to the reign of Hazrat Khalīfah Ilāhī (the August Representative of God on earth, viz., the Emperor Akbar) that bull was at the Gate of Delhi. The writer of this History [Khwājah Nizāmu'd-Dīn] has seen it.[59]

It seems that there was a Śiva Temple in the Bādalgarh outwork, most likely on the northern side of the Gūjarī-Mahal where large-scale ruins are still extant, and when the Lodi forces captured this outwork, the brazen Nandī was the most wonderful prize of this victory. Nizāmu'd-Dīn's account shows that the Bādalgarh complex was built by Raja Mansingh. This is more than confirmed by the style of the *Hindola-Paur* and the *Gūjarī-Mahal.*

Mullah 'Abdul Qādar Badāonī who wrote *Muntakhābu't-Tawārīkh* a little later, confirmed Nizāmu'd-Dīn's narrative, though he added:

The fortress of Badalgarh which lies below the fortress of Gwalior, a very lofty structure, was taken from Raja Mansingh and fell into the hands of the Muslims and a brazen animal which was worshipped by the Hindus also fell into their hands and was sent by them to

Agra, whence it was sent by Sultan Ibrahim to Delhi and was put up over the city-gate. This image was removed to Fathpur in the year 992 H. (=A.D. 1584), ten years before the composition of this history, where it was seen by the author of this work. It was converted into gongs and bells and implements of all kinds.[60]

Ferishtah who compiled his history during Jehangir's reign repeated the narrative of the *TA*.[61] Abdullah too who wrote his *Tarikh-i-Daudi* also during Jehangir's reign, exactly reproduced its narrative.[62] Aḥmad Yādgār who also wrote during Jehangir's time, repeated it with some alterations, that it was a copper bull which used to speak by itself and the sultan placed it at the Agra Fort where it remained until Akbar ordered it to be melted and a cannon was made of it.[63]

Gūjarī-Mahal is an integral part of the Badalgarh out-work, situated inside it at the foot of the rock-fort on its north-east corner. Militarily it occupies an extremely weak position; with practically no defences it could be easily taken. It seems, therefore, that Raja Mansingh built this palace before the Lodi menace precipitated. Possibly, the palace was built contemporaneously to the Man-Mandir, *c.* 1500, and the Badalgarh out-work was added later to defend it. The ruined structures situated to the north of the Gūjarī-Mahal definitely belong to an earlier period and they tend to show that the Tomar structures flourished on this site even before the accession of Raja Mansingh. The brazen Nandī which has been mentioned by Muslim historians might have belonged to an ancient or early medieval Śivālaya.

The Gūjarī-Mahal palace (Plate LXIX) has a square plan. The ground floor is at present entirely closed except for a 'Talghar (basement complex) in the centre of the plan, comprised of a double-storeyed set of rooms and verandahs, and a long, through corridor on the western side. It is not the plinth of the palace, as it appears. Though exteriorly the ground floor is closed on all sides, basement apartments and the western corridor show that this too was a full-fledged storey, probably divided into two sub-storeys, which had halls and rooms and inter-connecting corridors and stairways. All this has now been closed up and remains a mystery.

The upper storey (first floor) is accessible through a broad comfortable stairway provided in the centre of the southern side. Originally there was an entrance on the northern side too, but this has now been closed up. Both are private in nature. The southern entrance has a beautiful lintel and elephant-brackets doorway with a graceful sculpture, that of a door-keeper (pratihāra) on its either side (Plate LXX). Over it, slightly to the west, is a double-storeyed oriel-window. The upper one contains a large stone sculpture of an elephant which faces west (Plate LXXI). There is a similar composition over the northern (closed) entrance of the palace with an exactly similar sculpture but, curiously, this elephant faces east. This is something mysterious. Certainly, there was a serious meaning behind the setting of the two elephants in opposite directions but now this is not known. Each one stands over the entrance, on either side of the palace, guarding it imposingly. That the sculpture of an elephant is placed over the gate inside an oriel-window just like a show-piece is also an unusual feature of an architecture.

As it stands at present, the *Gūjarī-Mahal* is a large open courtyard around which, on all sides, oblong rooms and verandahs have been given which now house the famous 'Gujari Mahal Museum' under the M.P. State Department of Archaeology. There are a few larger apartments also which have ribs-and-panels and wagon-vaulted ceilings. It is all stone-work with a uniform system of construction. Brackets-and-lintel entrance and a flat ceiling are its characteristic features. The whole of it is utterly simple and unadorned; in fact, the interior has been so overwhelmingly converted to modern needs that there are no traces of any applied decoration and only the structure has remained.

The exterior, on the other hand, has not been disturbed and it has retained much of its original impression. The three facades, i.e., on the southern, eastern and northern sides, have been very gorgeously treated. The plain wall is relieved by a series of string-courses and cornices, which continue and rotate on all the three sides. A beautiful design in stone relief, resembling spear-headed cresting, is given at the first storey height. At the second storey height is an extremely slanting chhajja which is supported on regularly disposed, beautiful bracket-forms composed of elephant mouths. It looks to bear the beam on its tusk which has been raised in the effort to take it over and the sculpture is vigorous and lively. This elephant-bracket form is indeed an extremely beautiful composition, as are the vyāla and śārdūla brackets of the Man-Mandir. The chhajja also rotates on all the three sides and relieves the plain wall extremely magnificently (Plates LXXII and LXXIII). The broad frieze above it is divided into several horizontal zones which have carved and glazed-tiled designs. Most impressive is the haṁsāvali, the series of haṁsas, which though carved in stone have been done with mosaic of blue and yellow glazed-tiles; they give an extraordinary lustrous impression to the facade. Haṁsāvali has been used here in exactly the same way and with exactly the same effect as

on the *Man-Mandir* and it confirms that both were built contemporaneously or, at the most, Gūjarī-Mahal followed the Man-Mandir in
quick succession. Parapet is protected by a cresting of arch-shaped
merlons. Noteworthy is the form of the arch which is emphatically ogee
in distinct contravention to the typically Muslim type. The whole of the
facade on each side has been judiciously treated so as to associate carved
and glazed-tiled ornaments with adequate plain surfaces which automatically take the eye above to the beautifully adorned superstructure.

The pavilions of the *Gūjārī-Mahal* which make up most of the
beautiful effect of its superstructure are unique in the whole range of
medieval art. At the corners, it is a double-storeyed structure (Plate
LXXIV) which is a balcony (gaukh), an oriel (jharokha) and a cluster
of chhatris—at one and the same time. The jharokhas in both storeys
are closed with typical Tomar jalis which are in fact plain thin sheets
of stone having only simple partial perforations. Beautiful peacock-
shaped struts which are entirely ornamental have been used with the
chhajjas protecting the lower jharokhas. A few jalis of the upper
jharokhas have been removed. The spherical cupolas of these oriels
flank the dome of the main chhatri extremely impressively. Each one
is crowned by āmalaka-and-kalaśa finial. In the centre of the eastern
side is a similar jali-closed jharokha. In this case, however, graceful
serpentine struts have been used instead of peacock-shaped struts
(Plate LXXV). Here also its cupola rests on the skyline along with the
dome of the main chhatri, almost as if the former is reposing in the
shade of the latter. That the architect of the palace devoted such a
great thought to devise these features with a view to bring about an
exquisite architectural effect is a remarkable feature of this composition. No doubt, the jharokhas could have been used by the inmates of
the palace for fresh-airing, and enjoying vistas and views, but their
provision on the superstructure has been mainly guided here by
aesthetic consideration.

The most important aspect of the Gūjarī-Mahal palace is the Arabic
and Persian epigraph which has been carved and glazed-tiled upon the
frieze of the window-opening above the southern entrance. It is in two
lines. The first line is Arabic which reads:

"Bismillah-al-Rehman-al-Rahim Al-Mulko-Lillah
Malik-ul Mulq Zul-Jalal"

(The country belongs to God who is the Supreme Lord of the
Universe; He sustains it.)

The verse itself is not Quranic; it is an adaptation of the Quranic dictum Sura LXVII Verse 1 which reads: "Blessed be He (God) in whose hand is dominion and He over all things hath power."[64] Second line is Persian which reads:

"In-dua-e madad-in ki Rajah Mansingh bin Rajah Kalyanmal"

(This palace was built by the blessings of Raja Mansingh, son of Raja Kalyanmal.)

The incidence of the use of (i) an Arabic-Persian epigraph on the palace-gateway and (ii) its depiction in such a typically Muslim ornamental scheme as glazed-tiling is an extraordinary feature of this palace. The whole of it belongs to the fabric of the structure and also coincides with the spirit of its glazed-tile ornamentation and there is no doubt that it was done, *in situ*, contemporaneously to the palace. There is no reason to suppose that somebody did it later under the Great Mughals who succeeded the Tomars in the possession of the Fort. Nobody would have liked to do it and, had somebody decided to inscribe something like this, he would have certainly, almost as a rule, used the name of the ruling Mughal emperor therein. This is not there.

Why the raja chose to use the Arabic-Persian inscription, in glazed-tiling with a Muslim invocation, instead of the Hindu: 'Om Namo Vasudevāya', over the entrance of his palace is an important question. There may be many surmises but there is nothing on record to sustain any hypothesis. Allied with this question is also the problem of its nomenclature: Gūjarī-Mahal. There is no contemporary record to support it and it is only the legend which names this palace as such. The legendary version further holds that the raja built this palace for the residence of his most beloved queen who was of the Gūjar tribe and came from the village Rāī, because she would not live in the Fort along with his other queens in the traditional royal way. There may be a lot of truth in the legend which has survived intact, but in the absence of any documentary evidence to corroborate it, it is not safe to rely on it for writing the history of the palace. Narayandas would have certainly alluded to the exceedingly interesting romance of the raja with the Gūjar damsel in a village setting in his *CC*. There is no mention whatsoever. It may be admitted, however, that the nomenclature of the palace owes its origin to her.[65]

The Arabic-Persian epigraph is vitally related to the question of Raja Mansingh's sovereignty. It is noteworthy, in this connection, that all his inscriptions which mention him as Mahārājādhirāja (and are all in Nāgarī) are limited to the Fort and we do not come across any epigraph or land-grant or consecration-tablet of the raja outside it. That he was ever coronated and possessed the paraphernalia of sovereignty as prescribed by the śāstras is not on record. The Persian chronicles give an altogether different version. Also significant in this respect is the fact that the Lodi coinage called 'Bahlolī' was in currency at Gwalior itself and no coin of the raja has come to light so far. The Gūjarī-Mahal inscription furnishes an important clue to the Tomar polity.[66]

Immediately attached to the *Gūjarī-Mahal* on its northern side are a number of palatial ruins. Sets of pillared verandahs and halls were given on all the four sides of a spacious stone-paved courtyard. They were double-storeyed structures. All this is simple stone-work with little carving or any other ornament. A basement storey was also there and a room with spherical soffit and a tunnel of this complex have survived intact. A number of stairways sunk into the depth of walls interconnected the various apartments in several storeys. On the south-western corner of this ruined palace is situated a huge baoli which was probably the main source of water-supply of the Fort. Traces of several channels which ran into different directions have survived. A deep, square, masonry storage tank situated close to the northern entrance of the *Gūjarī-Mahal* also drew its water from the baoli. However, this has all been long in disuse and defunct, and it is not possible to reconstruct its plan at present.

The *Hindola-Paur* is also an imposing gateway which introduces the visitor to the Badalgarh complex in as befitting a manner as the *Hathiya-Paur* stands in relation to the *Man-Mandir*. The arched entrance, which has a beautiful fringe of stylised spear-heads along its intrados and a similar motif at the apex, is flanked on either side by an oriel-window with mañchikā base, and a circular tower crowned by the typical Tomar chhatri of similar circular conformation having a similar round balustrade and chhajja (Plate LXXVI). The towers bear several carved and glazed-tiled designs, the most prominent being, again, the typical series of swans, viz., the haṁsāvali which has been carved and glazed-tiled. This too is exactly similar to the series which appear on the *Gūjarī-Mahal* and the *Man-Mandir*. The entrance arch is a true (radiating) arch with large, stone voussoirs and a huge keystone which bears the stylised spear-head design (i.e., at the apex). Both the external and internal arches are similar. The internal arch is flanked by miniature ornamental oriel-windows which are set on an otherwise plain facade extremely beautifully (Plate LXXVII). Though this gateway has been designed in accordance with the defence needs of the time, it goes to the credit of the architect that he also gave it substantial aesthetic character. It is this way that physical needs were reconciled with the aesthetic tastes of the people and ornamentation went hand in hand with functional architecture. The Mughals, from Babur to Akbar, must have noticed this feature with admiration and of course with obligation.

Characteristic Features of Raja Mansingh Tomar's Style [67]

This study of the *Man-Mandir* and the *Gūjarī-Mahal* palaces helps us to deduce the characteristic features of Raja Mansingh Tomar's architectural style, which may be summarised as follows.

(1) Stone (which was locally available in great quantity) in a wide variety of tints and tones, mainly being grey, yellow and white sand-stone, is the building material of these palaces. Even when skeleton is made up of rubble or ashlar, facings have been done in dressed and polished stone. Generally, the skeleton-blocks themselves have made the facings, like the construction of the Hindu temple. There is no brick and the typical Tomar palaces have no plaster-work. This helps us to distinguish the original Tomar buildings from the later constructions, conversions and restorations.

(2) The palaces have been laid out with an inner courtyard in the centre of the plan and a smaller court in each annexe, around which rooms and halls have been disposed in two storeys. These apartments invariably open on the courtyard. Adequate arrangement of light and air has been made in them. Originally, provision of a number of water-devices was also made. The plan of these palaces in multiple storeys has been so disposed as to provide them with an efficient system of interconnecting corridors, secret passages and stairways, which receive their light and air through long overflying ventilators.

(3) It is mainly the trabeate (horizontal) system of construction, with overall emphasis on pillars and beams. Such trabeate features as kadalikā-karaṇa (corbelling), mañchikās (seats with lotus-shaped bases), āsanas (seats with slanting slabs), jharokhas (oriels), toraṇas, chhajjas, brackets and struts have been used on a large scale. The load is generally sought to be supported on the traditional horizontal system of the Hindus. True arch with voussoirs is rare but a large number of

arcuate ceilings have been used to roof the halls, and vault and dome are as characteristic of this art as is the flat ceiling. Some ceilings of the *Man-Mandir* are unique compositions. The new inspiration of construction has been marvellously used along with the indigenous technique.

(4) However, many of the structural features, as vyāla-brackets, struts, āsanas, mañchikās etc., have been used mainly ornamentally. Once the problem of supporting a load on the beam-and-post system was solved, the architect was free to use all subsidiary features to impart the structure an aesthetic impression as best as he could.

(5) Stone being the building material, carving and sculpturesque decor is the chief mode of ornamentation. With this indigenous art, typical Muslim colour scheme of glazed-tiling has been gorgeously combined. Polychrome surface ornament is beautifully set with the stone relief and this is a unique phenomenon of the art of these 15th century palaces. It raises many questions. How did it appear at Gwalior? Was it an attempt of the liberal raja to contribute to the development of a composite style of art? What was the source of his inspiration? Who did it for him? Was the glazed-tiler of these palaces a Muslim from Sindh, the traditional home of this art during the Sultanate period, or an indigenous artisan from Gujarat or Mandu? The excellent way in which he has expressed this art in terms of indigenous idioms shows that, whatever was the case, the glazed-tiler of Gwalior belonged, probably through several generations, to the soil and climate of the country and the overtones of the art had been Indianised. Noteworthy is the fact that his polychrome is always composed with stone-relief in carving and is never on a plain surface; tiles have been set in mosaic, direct on the stone surface without any associated plaster-work.

(6) Certain animal-forms have been used here predominantly, viz., makara, haṁsa, siṁha (lion), hastīn (elephant), mayūra (peacock), śārdūla and vyālas (composite animals). All stone-carved, they are motifs of indigenous art.

(7) Side by side with these forms, typically Muslim geometrical, arabesque and stylised designs have also been used. Some are carved and jalied, but they are mostly glazed-tiled.

(8) Jalis have also been used on a very large scale and this art occupies an important position in its ornamental scheme. Both simple and complicated designs have been used. Geometrical and foliated designs predominate in this scheme. Parapet jalis are unique. It is noteworthy that jali-art is a later development in India. Jālī (jālaka) has

not been mentioned in the *Viṣṇudharmottara-Purāṇa* (*c.* 650 A.D.), or *Samarāṅgaṇa-Sūtradhāra* of Raja Bhoja (*c.* 1025), or *Aparājitapṛchchhā* of Bhuvanadevāchārya (*c.* 1200), or *Vāstu-Sāra-Prakaraṇa* of Thakkur Pheru (*c.* 1315). It is only later that jalis came into popular usage and, consequently, they found mention in the texts. Thus *Kāśyapa-Śilpa* (*c.* 1450) and *Śilpa-Ratnam* of Śrīkumāra (*c.* 1600) have a chapter each on Jālaka-Lakṣaṇam,[68] the latter following almost ad verbatim the former. They described six types of jali-designs:

गोनेत्रं हस्तिनेत्रं च नन्द्यावर्तं ऋजुक्रियम् ।
पुष्पकर्णं सकर्णं च जालकं षड्विधं भवेत् ॥

(KS, XI, 9)

Simple geometrical designs made up of straight lines and foliated designs are conceived under this prescription. But there is no provision for stylised designs or arabesques. Jali has been used on a very large scale in Gujarat, first in wood and then in stone, and it became a distinctive characteristic of its art during the 15th century. It seems that Gujarat provided the earliest source of inspiration of this art and Gwalior is also indebted to it for this inspiration, though it is likely that it travelled over such a vast distance through Mewar. The parapet-jalis of the Man-Mandir, with elephant and lion forms perforated into them, bear a distinct Rajasthani influence. In such a hot region as Gwalior, and in a 15th century composite society when purdah had come into vogue, it was an enormously useful architectural expedient.

(9) Treatment of the facade is also a special feature of this style. Each facade has been divided into several zones and planes, horizontal lines being harmoniously counterbalanced by the verticality of the towers. Several pleasing series, e.g., toraṇāvali, haṃsāvali and makarāvali, which combine stone relief art with the lustre of polychrome glazed-tiles, are beset gorgeously in them. Openings are generally given by balconies (gaukhs) and oriels (jharokhas) which break the surface monotony extremely impressively.

(10) The Tomar architect was also master of superstructure which he knew well to manipulate to the best ideals of the architectonic effect. He used chhatris, gaukhs, jharokhas, chhaparkhats and other pleasing features to create a beautiful skyline.

(11) A number of folk-elements used in the Tomar architecture also constitute a characteristic feature of this art. Apart from the stylised forms of chhatri (pillared pavilion), gaukh (balcony) and jharokha (oriel), the following have also been used:

(i) Khaprel design—in the chhajjas of interior courts;
(ii) Biṭaurā-form—in the cupola shapes and also independently;
(iii) Chhaparkhat-form—on the superstructure; and
(iv) Chhappar (slanting thatched-hut roof) form—in the ceilings.

As a whole, the Tomar architecture of Gwalior, of which *Man-Mandir* is the most representative example, is composed of changed structural expedients and ornamental themes and it shows a spirit of eclecticism; it marks the beginning of the formation of a composite style which, even at this early stage, is national in character.

REFERENCES

1. It is true, as Dr Pramodchandra has observed, that "The use of terms like 'Renaissance' and 'Neo-Classic' which have come to possess a very fixed, specific range of meaning and ideas in the English language may not be always applicable to the Indian situation." It has been used here in the sense of movement of rejuvenation and revival of the old order of things, full of vigorous artistic and intellectual activity, which lasts an epoch, age or a period.

2. See *Appendix*-A for a List of Great Contemporaries of Raja Mansingh Tomar of Gwalior.

3. Unfortunately it is no longer available and we know of it only through Faqirullah's *Rāga-Darpaṇa* which he compiled in 1073/1671, cf. H.N. Dwivedi, *Mansingh aur Man-Kutoohal* (Hindi) (Gwalior, v.s. 2010).

4. For a few details of these inscriptions, see S.L. Katare, 'Two Gangolatal Gwalior Inscriptions of the Tomara Kings of Gwalior', *Journal of Oriental Institute*, Baroda, Vol. XXIII, No. 4 (June 1974). Two other inscriptions belonged to Raja Mansingh Tomar, as discussed hereafter. It is unfortunate that they were not recovered and again sank into 40' water.

5. *BN*, p. 611.

6. *Briggs*, Vol. I, p. 119.

7. Ibid., p. 119.

8. *ASI*, Cun. II, p. 381; another inscription of a mosque built by him has recently been discovered by this author.

9. Barni, *E&D*, Vol. III, p. 217; *Rehla*, pp. 43-45.

10. *Rehla*, p. 45.

11. Nearly all the Jaina caves around the Fort were excavated and their beautiful images and sculptures were also carved during the pre-Mansingh period from 1440 to 1473.

12. This is attested by the Dhondha-Paur inscription; see *Appendix*-B for its text at the end of this chapter.

13. See *Appendix*-B for text.

14. Above the names is a carved panel which bears a hand pointing towards east. This is a mysterious sign.

15. A large number of loose and carved sculptures and inscriptions engraved on the bed were found when the Gangola-Tal was cleaned and desilted by the Sikhs recently. The Ek-Khambha Tal, the Rani-Tal and the Cheri-Tal have never been cleaned and it is certain that their water and mud conceal a lot of valuable material of historical importance. The Archaeological Survey of India should take inspiration and directive from the Gangola-Tal example.

16. See *Appendix*-C for the text. Major portion of this epigraph is unintelligible.

17. *BN*, pp. 607, 610.

18. Ibid., p. 613.

19. *ASI*, Cun. II, p. 396.

20. Cunningham mentioned another inscription of Humayun in the Fort dated in the same year, i.e., 938/1531 (cf. op. cit., II, 396), but this too has been lost.

21. *BN*, 607-11.

22. This is indicated by Cunningham in his plan of these palaces, cf. *ASI*, Cun. II, Plate LXXXVII. The arrangement has since been entirely disturbed; not only alterations have been made, a large number of structures shown in Cunningham's

plan around 1862 have also been demolished and the ground cleared.

23. As regards paucity of material for writing the history of the Tomars of Gwalior, the author's paper 'On the Sovereignty of Raja Mansingh Tomar of Gwalior', *Journal of Oriental Institute*, Baroda (Vol. 28, No. 1, September 1978) would be an interesting and useful reading.

24. *BN*, 607.

25. This leaves no doubt that it was the *Man-Mandir* which has been described by Babur.

26. Originally, the palace covered an area $300' \times 160'$ in size, a large part of which is now in ruins.

27. Traces of a thin over-coat of plaster were noticed by Cunningham, *ASI* Cun. II, 349.

28. Ibn Batutah (*Rehla*, op. cit., p. 45) noticed only one mahout. But his narrative generally lacks precision and is erroneous at times. Babur's account, in any case, is more reliable.

29. *BN*, 607-11.

30. The *Chhitai-Charit* of Narayandas (ed. by H.N. Dwivedi and Agarchand Nahta, Gwalior, 1960).

31. See *Appendix*-D for the text of Narayandas.

32. This is poetic fantasy. The glazed-tiling was a different process. This author's *Colour Decoration in Mughal Architecture* (Taraporevala, Bombay, 1970), pp. 12-14 may be referred to for details.

33. *CC*, chaupais 113-131, pp. 15-17.

34. Cf. *History of Indian and Eastern Architecture*, Vol. II (revised by James Burgess) (New Delhi, 1967), p. 176. He continues in fn. 3, "We occupied the fort during the mutiny and retained it long after. The first thing done was to occupy the Baradari as a mess-room; to fit up portions of the palace for military occupation; then to build a range of barracks, and *clear away a lot of antiquarian remains to make a parade ground*. What all this means is only too easily understood." He further quoted M. Rousselet from his *L'Inde des Rajahs* to lay emphasis upon this point.

35. Cf. *Famous Monuments of Central India* (London, 1886), pp. 57-58.

36. *ASI*, Cun. II, Plate LXXXVII.

37. Cunningham's various measurements of the Man-Mandir Palace (vide *ASI*, Cun. II, Plate LXXXVII) are not correct. Thus he gives $33' \times 33'$ as the size of this court. This author physically measured it $34'-9'' \times 36'-6''$. It seems that there were additional walls or other similar subsidiaries during the period from 1844 to 1849 when Cunningham resided in the Fort and took these measurements. In any case, this author has not followed Cunningham and he has taken his own measurements.

38. It is a gaja-vyāla in accordance with the Śilpa-text:
इति षोडश व्यालानि उक्तानि मुख-भेदतः
(*AP*, 233.6) (cf. *Aparājita-pṛchchhā*, ed. P.A. Mankad, G.O.S. No. 115, Baroda, p. 595). For a similar study of vyālas at the Agra Fort, reference may be made to the author's 'Depiction of Fabulous Animals— Gaja-Vyāla at the Delhi-gate of Agra Fort' (*Medieval India: A Miscellany*, Aligarh, Vol. 2, 1972). Reference may also be made to his paper 'On the Gateways of Chanderi' (*Indo-Iranica*, Calcutta, Vol. 30, Nos. 3-4, Sept-Dec 1977).

39. *CC*, op. cit., pp. 16-17.

40. *BN*, 607.

41. Lepel Griffin (cf. *Famous Monuments of Central India*, London, 1886, p. 51) has recorded, around 1886, to have seen, on the southern

facade, such figures: "They have representations of men holding chowries and all in the same charming tile-work." But they are not traceable at present.

42. For a detailed study of the 'Chhaparkhat' reference may be made to the author's paper 'Notice on Firoz Shah's Reference to CHHAPARKHAT in the Futūḥat-i-Fīrozshāhī' (*Journal of the Asiatic Society*, Calcutta, in press).

43. The editors also give the alternate reading: 'खटछपर' ।

44. *CC*, op. cit., p. 16.

45. Ibid., p. 17.

46. Ibid., p. 17.

47. Ibid., p. 16.

48. Ibid., p. 16.

49. For details of this study, reference may be made to the author's *Colour Decoration in Mughal Architecture*, op. cit., pp. 12-14.

50. *CC*, op. cit., p. 15.

51. Percy Brown is not fair and just when he noted in this connection: "Viewed as a whole, therefore, this palace while on the one hand a representative example of decorative architecture is, on the other hand, also an exceptional type of architectural decoration, and its fault lies in the fact that its designers attempted too much in their effort to fulfill both objects" (cf. *Indian Architecture*, Islamic period, p. 127). It is a pity that Brown mostly wrote at Calcutta without actually personally seeing and studying all the monuments he described in an impressive and inimitable language, of which he was certainly a master. He spread the vast data, received from the Archaeological Survey of India and other sources, on the canvas and painted it through the colourful words and phrases into a beautiful composition the literary merit of which indeed remains unexcelled, without worrying for the historical aspect of his narrative, which is tremendously impoverished due to lack of first-hand knowledge. Unless one actually resides in the region and with the monuments which he ventures to interpret, the spirit of an architectural style is easily missed!

52. *Rehla*, pp. 45, 163.

53. *BN*, 609.

54. *Ain*, II, p. 181.

55. Ibid., p. 180; in fact, it is the western gate (and not eastern). It is also called the Delhi-Gate. It was completed in 1568-69. For details of this gateway reference may be made to the author's *Some Aspects of Mughal Architecture* (New Delhi, 1976), pp. 49-53.

56. *Ain*, II, p. 180.

57. See, for details of this matter, author's paper 'The Diwan-i-Khas of Fatehpur Sikri: A Symbol of Akbar's Belief in Sūrya-Puruṣa', cf. *Some Aspects of Mughal Architecture*, op. cit., pp. 7-21.

58. *TA*, I, 401.

59. Ibid., pp. 402-3; thus it was at Delhi *c.* 1593.

60. *MT*, I, 432-33.

61. *Briggs*, I, 347-48.

62. Cf. *UTKB*, I, 297.

63. Cf. ibid., p. 343. It is this curious way that the historians of medieval India followed one another, borrowed the things from their predecessors and fancifully added to the narrative—to make history romantic!

64. *HQ*, p. 1576.

65. Vrindabanlal Verma's Hindi novel *Mṛganayanī* is an excellent piece of literature; it is unfortunate that most of its fiction has, almost unconsciously, filtered into the Tomar history. That the raja arranged to bring the Rāī-water to the Fort for

the use of the Gujar queen, for instance, is a romantic imagination of the novelist, rather than a documented fact of history.

66. For a few details of this matter, reference may be made to the author's paper 'On the Sovereignty of Raja Mansingh Tomar of Gwalior', *Journal of the Oriental Institute*, Baroda (Vol. 28, No. 1, September 1978).

67. With its set norms and principles, STYLE is an evolutionary process which gradually grows and develops and ultimately reaches the stage of perfection at which these norms and principles are perceptibly symbolised. An independent style can be studied with regard to four basic aspects, viz., (i) lay-out and plan of buildings, (ii) structural contrivances employed, (iii) ornamental themes adopted, and, above all, (iv) adjustment of usage and functional necessity with symbolic, ceremonial and, most important, aesthetic outlook of the builders—which, altogether, constitute its distinctive characteristics marking the whole evolutionary process.

68. *Kāśyapa-Śilpa* (ed. V.G. Apte) (Anand Ashram Sanskrit Series, No. 95, Poona, 1926), Chapter XI, pp. 32-33 and *Śilpa-Ratnam* (ed. T. Ganapati Sastri) (Trivandrum Sanskrit Series, No. 75, Trivandrum, 1922), pp. 142-43.

APPENDIX-A

**Great Contemporaries of Raja Mansingh Tomar
of Gwalior
(1486-1516)**

Bhakti Saints	*Kings of Sovereign States*
1. Kabir (*c.* 1450-1518)	1. Sikandar Lodi of Delhi (1487-1517)
2. Nanak (1469-1538)	2. Kumbha (1433-68) and Sanga (1509-28) of Mewar
3. Vallabha (1478-1530)	3. Mahmud Begarha of Gujarat (1458-1511)
4. Chaitanya (1485-1533)	4. Ghiyathud-Din Khalji of Malwa (1469-1500)
5. Mirabai (1498-1546)	5. Mahmud Bahmani (1482-1518)
	6. Krishna Devaraya of Vijayanagar (1509-29)

APPENDIX-B

Inscriptions of Raja Mansingh Tomar in the Gwalior Fort

(a) *Inscription on a Jaina Image on the Fort* (v.s. 1552/A.D. 1495)

श्रीमऊ गोपाचलगढ़ दुर्गे ।। महाराजाधिराज
श्रीमल्ल (मान)सिंह देवराज्ये प्रवर्त्तमाने संवत
१५५२ वर्षे ज्येष्ठसुदि————[1]

(b) *Inscription on the Dhvajastambha facing the Larger Sas-Bahu Temple* (1545/1488)

सिद्धि संवत् १५४५ वध्वो फाल्गुन
वदि २ — लिषिते पेगोमनु । —
लिष——त————[2]

(c) *Inscription in the Sas-Bahu Temple* (carved on the pavement slab of western upper storey, along with several motifs, yantras and diagrams) (1553/1496)

सतोषाला —रा—मान—व्रान्तिकेत्रेमहीपाल-प्रयतु १५५३ पौषे —ऋषि सुदि —२ गुरु————[3]

(d) *Inscription at the Dhondha-Paur* (in the niche of the Dhondha-Deva) (1552/1495)

सिधि (सिद्ध) संवतु १५५२ वर्षे ग्रसुनिसुर
महाराजाधिराज राजा श्रीमान ।।
सांघ (सिंह) देवधिरंराजे साटोवर ।।
ढोढादेव मूर्त्तिकारापितं ।।
लि॰ साजसू सूत्रयारि (सूत्रधारि) महमे ।।
गढंत धरमनन्दु ।। नाथू हुपदास

1. Purnachand Nahar, *Jain Shilalekha*, Part II (1927), p. 93, Inscription No. 1429.
2. There are other inscriptions on this stambha but they are mostly unintelligible. It seems that these inscriptions record the restoration of the structures upon which they appear, under the raja.
3. This also seems to record restoration of the temple by the raja.

ढोढा की पौरि राजा
मानसाहि नईा (ई) कराई (ई)
प्रकरीण्ड ॥

(e) *Inscription at the Urwahi-Paur* (on the pilaster in the interior Dalan) (1553/1496)

॥ श्री ॥
॥ श्री लडसुप्रीतमान
॥ सिध (सिंह) श्री इष्टदेवता प्रशादात् ॥
॥ महाराजाधिराज राजा श्री
॥ मान सांघ (सिंह) देव चिरंजीवी
तस्य अ (आ)ज्ञाकारी साटो
॥ बर उरवाइी (ई) की पौरि
बईी (ड़ी) करवाई (ई) ॥ लि०
साजसू (मार्गेवारी ॥ तस्मा
म (त्) साराणासटिहा ढोढ़ा
सूत्रधारि महेसु ॥ गढ़ंत
सींघ वर्मा वंद ॥ सुलम
॥ सू ॥ १ संवत १५५३
वर्षे आसाढ़ सुदि १३
गुरुवासरे ॥ अनु
ना हा नु ह त्र
१ षेऊ सुत्रधारि ॥
ग्वालिरी हिंकमिति ॥[4]

(f) *Inscription of the Gangola-Tal* (1551/1494)

ॐ सिधि । श्रीगणेसायनमः । गोवर्धनगिरिवरं
करसाष एव । वित्रतूगवांमुपरिवारिघरार्दितानां ॥
बाल्येपि विस्मयन विधावल सच्चरित्रं । कृस्नश्रिस्तु
तत्र तोमर मानसिघः ॥ १ ॥ चिरंजीव चिरंनन्दा
चिरं पालयं ॥ ✕ ॥ मेदनी । श्री मानसिंह
राजेन्द्र जावच्चंद्र दिवाकरौ ॥ २ ॥

अथ संवत्सरेस्मिन् श्री विक्रमादीत्य राज्ये
संवत् १५५१ वर्षे वैसाष सुदि ३
मंगलवासरे । रोहिणी नक्षत्रे सौभाग्य नाम

---

4. The last word of this epigraph is not झिलमिली (jhilmili) as has been read, obviously with a preconceived notion, by H.N. Dwivedi at the behest of Mr Arthur Hughes, I.C.S. (cf. *Gwalior-ke-Tomar*, Gwalior, 1976, p. 379).

जोगे ।। श्री गोपाचल दुर्गे तोमरवंसे
महाराजाधिराज श्री मानसिंहदेव विजैंराज्ये ।।
तस्य प्रधान सरषषं मुलवार ज्ञातीय साह
षेमसाह श्री टोकर तसलीम साराण तेन
गंगोला तडागं निर्म्मली कृता । आचंन्द्रार्क
चिरंद्यातु । शुभं कल्यान्तं श्रियोस्तववु ।
लिखितं श्रीमाल ज्ञाती साजस ।। सूत्रधारि
पजू ।। श्री इष्ट देवताप्रसादास्तु ।। श्री ।। ।। श्री ।। ।। श्री ।।[5]

(g) *Inscription of the Gangola-Tal* (1551/1494)

सिंघे संवतु १५५१ वर्षे जेस्टवदे २ गूरजैंर
श्रीराजमानसीघदेवा वचनतु
पूथाना सटोजरामलगगेर सारयौ ।। राजा
की तसलिमा कामु जायैं ।।
सूत्रघरे पजू महलनं १ खीरसु १
मनूव १ सानेग १ रमा बढ़ई रमू
सिलहरी गने धनूत महं ।। चाढु १३ । ठूवल
सूवाकद्यो वोहरीत्र ।।[6]

5. This and the following inscription were found carved on the bed of the Gangola-Tal when it was cleaned and desilted by the Sikhs recently. The epigraphs were not recovered and again sank into water. The text is reproduced here from the stampages taken by Dr S.L. Katare and first printed by his consent by H.N. Dwivedi, op. cit., pp. 130-31.

6. There are a number of other epigraphs of Raja Mansingh in the fort. But they are fragmentary and unreadable; mostly they are carved in rock.

APPENDIX-C

Babur's Inscription dated v.s. 1586/A.D. 1529 in the Portal of the Chaurasi Khambha, Gwalior Fort

संवतु १५८६ वर्ष का——
बाव् (ब) (र) ना ् (नृ) पतिसहि (शाह) गजी तकेनज (?)
षोज (ख्वाजा) ना (र) हीम हह (दाद) कम हनस (?)
कनफुनाम (?) घी (बिन) अलह (अल्ला) दाद
षनासनौ———————

APPENDIX-D

Narayandas's Account of the Building of Man-Mandir
(Chhitai-Charit Text)
(महल-निर्माण)*

जे प्रवीन पाहन सुतधारा । वीरा दीनौ राइ हकारा ॥ ११३ ॥
कमठाने कहं आयसु भयो । अगनत दर्व काम लगि दयो ।
गुनी लंक गीगौ गुन दासू । जानहि सिलप ते बहुत अभ्यासू ॥ ११४ ॥
बोलि जोतिषी साधी लग्ना । रची नीव सुभनीके सगुना ।
खेत्रपालु पूजिउ करि भाउ । अविचल होउ ग्रेह द्रिठ राउ ॥ ११५ ॥
गही नीव भारी चौराई । पुरिष सात कइ मेरि भराई ।
चौबारे चउखंडि चौडोरा । कलिचा बने कांच के मोरा ॥ ११६ ॥
एकते काठन पाहन पाटे । नव नाटक नव साला ठाटे ।
नवीन रंग कुरि अति रवनीका । ठांव ठांव सोने के टीका ॥ ११७ ॥
बादल घनह उठी घन घटा । रचे अनूप अटारी अटा ।
छाजे भरोखा रचे अनूपा । जिन्हहि उभकिते रहे जे भूपा ॥ ११८ ॥
कठछपर सतखने अवासा । कंचन कलश मनहु कविलासा ।
रची केरि कांच की कडारी । रहिहि भूलि भ्रमु चतुर विचारी ॥ ११९ ॥
बावन वस्तु मिलइ कइ वानी । अति अनूप आरसी समानी ।
रची चित्रसारी चितलाई । देखत ही मनु रहिउ सिहाई ॥ १२० ॥
मानिकु चौक ते मन मोहनी । रची अनूप चोर मिहचनी ।
कीये भौंहरे अन अन भांती । तिनमहि जनि अंधियारी राती ॥ १२१ ॥
बने हिंडोरे कंचन खंभा । मानहु उपजे उकति सयंमा ।
करि सिगारु जे अधिक बिचारी । मानहु भरत की भरी सुनारी ॥ १२२ ॥
सभा जोरि जहं वइसइ राऊ । फटिक पीठ बंध्यो सो ठाऊ ।
चकई चकवा कीए कडारी । जल कूकर्रा मटामरियारी ॥ १२३ ॥
तिहठां और जिते जल जीवा । भरे भरति की साजति नींवा ।
मच्छ कच्छ लघु दीरघ घने । ते सब चलहि द्रिष्ट कर बने ॥ १२४ ॥
सभा सरोवर सोभइ तइसो । हथिनापुरि पांडव कउ जइसो ।
और राइ जे देखहि आई । वस न सकहि रहहि भरमाई ॥ १२५ ॥
चंदन काठ कठाइल आना । ते ग्रीषम रितु हेम समाना ।
चउबारे चउपखा सुदेसा । वरिखा बिरमइ तहां नरेसा ॥ १२६ ॥
सोने के पीपरि पंचासा । वरिखा वरखइं बारह मांसा ।
गोमट खरबूजा आकारा । तिन्हहि पवांरी जरे किवारा ॥ १२७ ॥

*Cf. *Chhitai-Charit* of Narayandas (ed. H.N. Dwivedi and Agarchand Nahta) (Gwalior, 1960), pp. 15-17 and 176-79.

चहुंघा खुटी कांच की भली । रहइ परेबा तहं जंगली ।
तिहं ठां सूवा सारो साखा । खुमरी बोलहिं अन अन भाखा ॥ १२८ ॥
एक महल नीर कौ दुराउ । दीसइं तह वइसन कौ ठांउ ।
देखति बुधि न होइ सरीरा । चलति बूड़ीयइ गहर गंभीरा ॥ १२९ ॥
हिलबी कांच भांति कइ करी । दीसइ जनु कालंद्री भरी ।
जिहं ठां राइ तणी जिउं नारा । दीसइ जमुना जल आकारा ॥ १३० ॥
जिनस जिनस मंदिरि गिन सारा । अरु सब ग्रेह बने इकसारा ।

PLATES

I.   Suraj Kund, Gwalior Fort

II.   Suraj Kund, Gwalior Fort

IV. Gwalior Fort

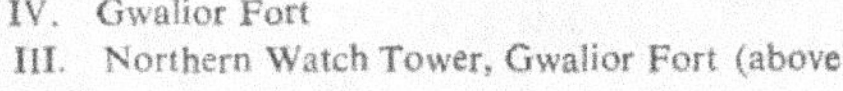
III. Northern Watch Tower, Gwalior Fort (above)

V. Urwahi Paur, Gwalior Fort

VI. Man-Sarovar,
     Gwalior Fort

VII. Man-Sarovar,
      Gwalior Fort

VIII. Rani Tal,
       Gwalior Fort

IX. Katora Tal, Gwalior Fort ↑

XI. Ek-Khambha Tal, Gwalior Fort →

X. Central Tower of the Katora Tal

XII. Central Pillar of the
      Ex-Khambha Tal

XIII. Iwan of the Chaurasi
       Khambha, Gwalior Fort

XIV. Step-Well of the Chaurasi Khambha, Gwalior Fort

XV. Pavilion near the Chaurasi Khambha, Gwalior Fort

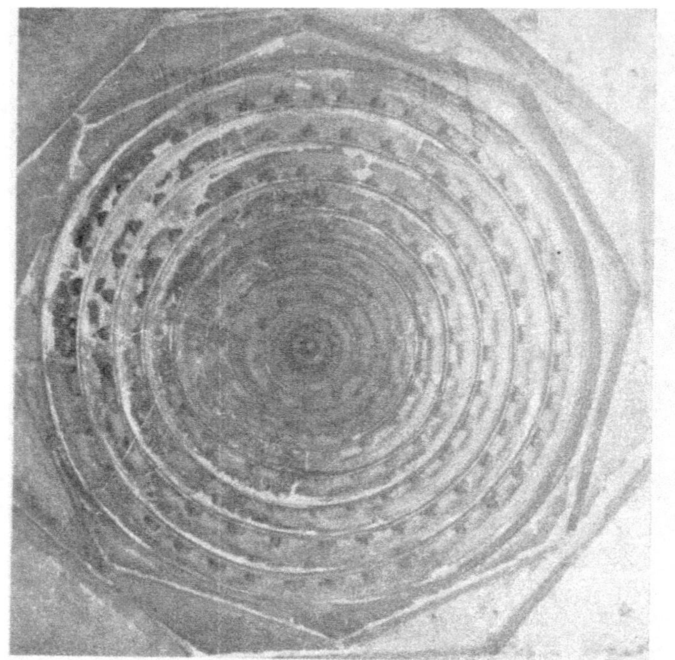

XVIII. Dome of the Eastern Porch

← XVII. Eastern Porch, Chaurasi Khambha

XVI. Vitāna of the Eastern Porch,
Chaurasi Khambha (above left)

XIX.   Arabic-Persian Inscription of the Chaurasi Khambha

XX.   Vikram Mahal, Gwalior Fort

XXI.   Eastern Facade of the Kirtti Mandir, Gwalior Fort

XXII.   Pair of Elephants, Gwalior Fort

XXIII. Northern Composition of the Kirtti Mandir, Gwalior Fort

XXIV. Western Facade of the Man Mandir, Gwalior Fort

XXV.   Pillar and Capital, Hall 'A' on Court 'X', Man Mandir

XXVI. Ceiling of the Hall 'A'

XXVII. Northern Facade of Court 'X'

XXVIII. Northern Facade of Court 'X'

XXIX. Ceiling of the Hall 'B'

XXX. Corridor attached to Hall 'B'

XXXI.   Western Facade of Court 'X'

XXXII.   Doorways of the Hall 'B'

XXXIII.   Doorways of the Hall 'B'

XXXIV.   Peacock Brackets of the Eastern Facade of Court 'X'

XXXV.   Vyāla Brackets of the Southern Facade of Court 'X'

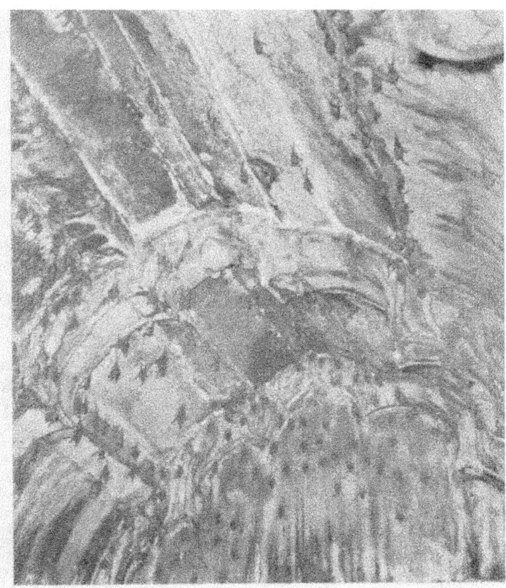

XXXVII.   Arched Ceilings of Room 'C'

↑ XXXVI.   Ceilings of the Hall 'D'

XXXVIII.   Ceilings of the Hall 'E'

XXXIX. Facade of the Hall 'F'

XLI. 'Khaprel' Type Chhajja of the Facade of the Hall 'F'

XL. Vyāla Brackets of the Facade of the Hall 'F'

XLII. Balcony of the Facade of the Hall 'F'

XLIII. Northern Facade of the Court 'Y'

XLV.   (a), (b) and (c) Vaulted Ceiling of the Hall 'G'

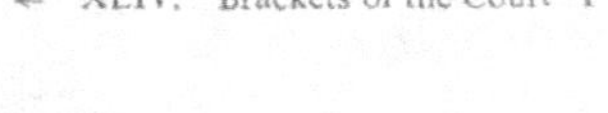

←   XLIV.   Brackets of the Court 'Y'

XLVI.   Wagon-vaulted Ceiling of the Hall 'H'

XLVII. Underground Passage,
Man Mandir

XLVIII. Ribs-and-Panels Ceiling Hall 'I'

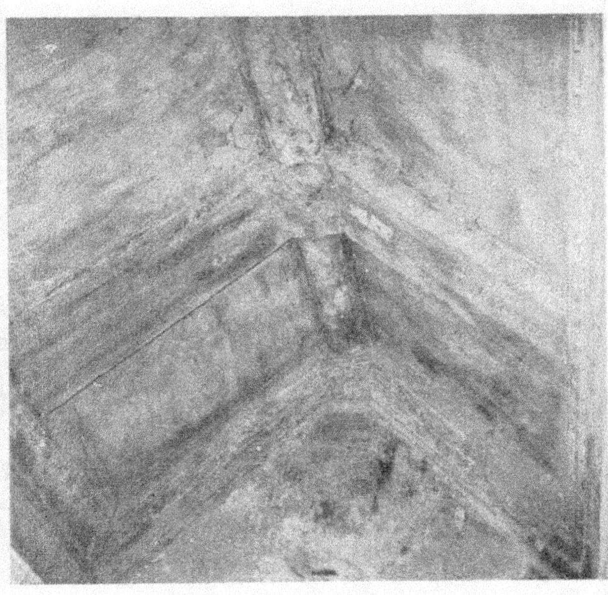

XLIX. Ribs-and-Panels Ceiling Hall 'J'

L.   Ribs-and-Panels Chhatris, Man Mandir

← LI.   Southern Facade with closed Chhatri,
        Man Mandir

LII.   Painting, Ceiling of the Chhatri

LIII. 'Chhaparkhat', Man Mandir

LIV. Oriel Window, Man Mandir →

LV. 'Bitaura' form Chhatri, Man Mandir

LVI. 'Bitaura' form Chhatri, Man Mandir →

← LVII.   Southern Facade of the Man Mandir

LVIII.   Southern Facade of the Man Mandir

LIX.   Makara Form at the Man Mandir

LXI.   Hathiya Paur, Man Mandir

←   LX.   Ogee Arch with Cusps, Man Mandir

LXIII.   Eastern Facade of the Man Mandir ↑

← LXIV.   Eastern Facade of the Man Mandir

LXII.   Painted Soffit of the Hathiya Paur (above left)

LXV.   Cornices and String-courses, Man Mandir

LXVI.   Through Corridor, Eastern Facade of Man Mandir

LXVII.   Skyline of the Man Mandir

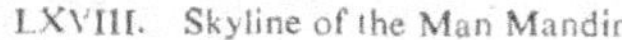

LXVIII.   Skyline of the Man Mandir

LXIX. Gujari Mahal Complex, Gwalior Fort

LXX. Southern Facade of Gujari Mahaᶥ,
Gwalior Fort

LXXI. Elephant Sculpture, Gujari Mahal

LXXII. Rotating Chhajja, Gujari Mahal

LXXIII. Chhajja and Elephant Brackets, Gujari Mahal

LXXIV. Corner Pavilion, Gujari Mahal

LXXV. Eastern Facade and Central 'Jharokha', Gwalior Fort

LXXVI. Tower of the Hindola Paur, Gwalior Fort

LXXVII. Hindola Paur